WOMAN IN CRISIS

OVERCOMING THE DEVASTATION OF MARITAL DISAPPOINTMENT

I0180248

BELLA ALEX-NOSAGIE

Beauty4Ashes12:30 Publishing

Dallas, Georgia

For information contact:
Beauty4Ashes 12 :30 Publishing, LLC
Dallas, Georgia 30157
beauty4ashes1230@aol.com
www.beauty4ashes1230.org

Book Cover design by SelfPubBookCovers.com/FrinaArt
Graphics and Back Cover design by Angie Zambrano

ISBN-13: 978-0692291238

I dedicate this book to:

God the Father, God the Son and God the Holy Spirit. You picked me up when I couldn't stand anymore. You wrapped your arms around me, when I was in despair. You have been there all my life watching and waiting for me to love you with all my heart, soul, mind and strength and you finally got my attention. Thank you for making my life relevant. Thank you for putting me on my path to destiny and finding my purpose because I was beginning to question the redundancy of my life. But through this pain you showed me the way. In 2013, on my birthday you touched me and activated the gifts within me for your Kingdom. A year later it is my birthday again, and as a measure of thanks this book is my present to you. Thank you for taking this book where it needs to go. To bring about a positive change in marriages and how people view their relationship with you. My life is yours, use me continually all my days. Thank you, Lord!

Contents

Acknowledgments

My Husband: Nosaa - Thank you for teaching me about unconditional love and forgiveness. With you I have learned what it truly means to be a Christian. A hard but necessary lesson in my journey to make Heaven. It is my prayer that you become all God has ordained you to be. I love you forever.

My Children: Jazmyn & Jaiden - You are my strength, you are my joy, and you are my song. You saved me in my darkest hour and continue to put the colors of the rainbow in my life when the sky threatens to be gray. Mommy loves you forever and always.

My Parents: Apostle Alexander Bamgbola & Rev.(Dr.) Grace Bamgbola - It is the nightmare of every parent to see their child hurt and cry at any age but you stood there for me. You repressed your hurt and anger and show love for my husband and I to this day. I thank you because from one parent to another I know it's no easy feat at all. You are truly servants of the most High God and I am proud to be your daughter. Thank you for encouraging me to step into my destiny and to do what God has called me to do. Love you Dad! Love you Mom!

My Brothers: David, Joseph & Samuel - Mom and Dad forgave it is my prayer that you do also. Know I am a better person for going through this. Know I discovered an aspect of my destiny in the process so it was not in vain. I appeal to you to love God fiercely, love your wives and always honor them. Great fathers beget wonderful daughters; do your part, and pray that your daughters grow into women who will love God fiercely because at the end of the day that is all that matters. I love you!

Special thanks to my Helpers of Destiny - Helpers of Destiny are people God puts in place to assist you on your path to destiny. Many times they are unaware they are your destiny helpers but you know it, especially once your purpose in life becomes clear. Therefore, I thank the following dearest people: Pastor Mike Adebiyi my beloved pastor. Pastor Deborah Babayemi my "Spiritual Mama", counselor and friend. Apostle Tim & Pastor Mrs Becky Atunnise words can't express what you both are to me and my family thank you so very much.

"My Person", Anne Alache Mark - When I was covered in shame you lifted me out of it with so much love, encouragement and laughter. You put me on my path to destiny by reminding me of an aspect of myself I had totally forgotten about. You said, "Bella, you are a Writer. Go and write!" Babe, this book exists today because God spoke through you and I listened. We've been friends since we were 11 years old never knowing it was a God ordained friendship. Words cannot describe what you mean to me I thank God for giving you to me as a "Best Friend Forever" and I am blessed to have found a sister in you. You are the epitome of what a Helper of Destiny is to me. God bless you and your precious family now and forever. Love you Annie!

And finally, to all women. We are stronger than the world gives us credit for. I wrote this for you!

Father, I pray for anyone who reads this book seeking healing in their marriage that you heal their "land" (2 Chronicles 7:14). I pray that anyone who is wondering what their destiny is, that you show them and help them walk in it. Father, I pray that whoever reads this book no matter their gender or marital status you empower them and strengthen them to do things according to your will in the name of Jesus. Amen.

~Introduction~

Ever wondered about that happy couple in the wedding photograph, their smiles forever captured in time? Here is the story behind that photograph. This is the true story of two imperfect people who came together as one, but yet to experience oneness only God's grace is sufficient. Marriage is hard and too many people are walking around pretending theirs is okay. This story will let you know that maybe yours isn't so bad. Maybe this will let you know yours is just as bad. And maybe this will be a piece of cake compared to what you have dealt with. After all I've only been married, as of today, 3 months shy of 5 years so what could I possibly teach you? I believe there is something to learn from every marriage. I hope you can learn from my experience. My mom described marriage to me shortly before my engagement ceremony as a package that comes with all kinds of things. Good, bad, ugly — you get it all. You don't get to open this package until you have said your vows. Then what do you do? How do you deal with it? The only way to survive is to develop a close and intimate relationship with God. He gives you the strength when you want to quit. He fills you with joy when you get no joy from your spouse. Devastating marriages happen every day but in Christianity it's a little bit more devastating. You take your vows with the best of intentions and promise to stick through thick and thin, but then something horrible goes wrong. Do you live up to your vows, or run away? Also, isn't life supposed to be much better if you marry within God's plan for you? Well, God's plan can throw you a curve ball in an effort to rebuild you into a new person and prepare you for your purpose and ministry. This is my story and this is my song. Read and be encouraged no matter what your situation is, God is always at work, and all you have to do is trust Him. God has sent me forth as a vessel to encourage you. I pray you will be encouraged and stand on God's promises. Trust Him in all seasons, His love never fails.

Then the word of the Lord came to me, saying: "Before I formed you in the womb I knew you; Before you were born I sanctified you; I ordained you a prophet to the nations." Then said I: "Ah, Lord God! Behold, I cannot speak, for I am a youth." But the Lord said to me: "Do not say, 'I am a youth,' For you shall go to all to whom I send you, And whatever I command you, you shall speak. Do not be afraid of their faces, For I am with you to deliver you," says the Lord. Then the Lord put forth His hand and touched my mouth, and the Lord said to me: "Behold, I have put My words in your mouth. See, I have this day set you over the nations and over the kingdoms, To root out and to pull down, To destroy and to throw down, To build and to plant" (Jeremiah 1:5-10).

1

The Age of Innocence

I was born September 14, 1982 in Cambridge, Massachusetts, U.S.A. but grew up in Lagos, Nigeria. My parents originally come from Nigeria and attended college in the U.S. They met each other and married in Boston. Dad, a career banker, was very brilliant and rose to becoming a vice president of The First National Bank of Boston. The family returned to Nigeria when my dad was sent by his employers to pioneer the formation of The First National Bank of Boston affiliate in Nigeria. My mom also picked up a banking career when they arrived in Nigeria, but had to give it up after a few years to raise the four children they were blessed with. I am the only daughter born to my parents. I have three brothers, two older and one younger. I love them to pieces. I am blessed to have been born into a great family of love.

I was always surrounded by men growing up and grew to be very comfortable with them. Ours was a big household of live-in maids, cooks, stewards, chauffeurs, and extended family. Things were never boring. It was when I became an adult I commended my parents for presenting an idyllic existence to their children even though their marriage was barely holding on. The main reason for this was mom and dad were not Christians when they married, but mom gave her life to Jesus Christ early on in the marriage. Whatever common ground they shared was now gone. I remember mom took the children from church to church on her quest to get closer to God. With the eyes of a child I thought it was typical behavior but now as a woman I totally understand what drove her to seek God tirelessly. *Do not be unequally yoked together with unbelievers. For what fellowship has righteousness with lawlessness? And what communion has light with darkness?* (2 Corinthians 6:14). I was deeply rooted in Christ from a young age. I knew no other way. Mom wouldn't even let me find another way, Jesus Christ was the only way. I remember giving my life to Jesus Christ at the age of six and at that young age I felt a call upon my life to sing. I told mom about it, and she informed the pastor of our local church and his wife that her daughter wanted to sing. I have no idea how an innocent request became such a big deal, because of God's favor upon my life I was allowed to join the adult choir. This had never been done in the history of the church, letting a child join the adult choir. It was a privilege and I was so happy. Everyone was nice to me, and I blended in quite nicely. I would sing tirelessly and be so thrilled to be there, singing was it for me! I stayed in the choir until I headed off to a Christian boarding school at the age of eleven in Plateau State, and there singing continued. When I reflect on it, the hand of God has always been on my life because His favor covered me wherever I went.

In this school a select few were chosen as Sunday school teachers, and I happened to be one of them. This was how I discovered another gift of mine — teaching the Bible — and I loved it. I remember I would get positive feedback from other students who passed through my Sunday school class, and it was rewarding serving God in this way. It was in boarding school I met a lifetime friend and what we now call a God ordained friendship, Anne Alache Jon Ode (now Anne Alache Mark). She was a very petite girl and I felt like a giant right next to her but she could sing and play the piano and I always admired that. She was smart as a whip too. We became close and I recorded a song on her tape recorder one day when we were tinkering around with music in school. Her dad happened to get ahold of it and heard my voice. Anne was working on an album to be produced by Panam Percy Paul, one of the gospel greats in Nigeria and she needed some extra voices to join her. Her dad heard my voice and suggested she bring me in on the project. I remember her family came over to my home and asked my parents' permission to have me on the project. That was such a happy day. I was so excited, and this brought Anne and me closer than ever. It was a privilege to meet and work with Panam Percy Paul. This was my first experience in a studio, and I loved the feel of it. I knew I belonged there. Just before I started what is the equivalent of the 11th grade in the U.S., my parents brought me back to Lagos to complete high school. They always planned to send all their children to the U.S. for college, and since I was turning into a young woman, they needed me at home to keep a closer eye on me and prepare me for the world in general. I wasn't too happy about it since I was quite popular in high school and now I was the new kid on the block. Being the new kid is never fun but eventually I became quite popular in my new school. Dad had given his life to Jesus Christ three years before I headed off to boarding school and he was now an assistant pastor in the church. However, he and mom were being led to start their own ministry, and in the summer of 1999 Zion the City of the Lord Ministries was born. That was the year I graduated from high school and I was heavily involved in the choir and whatever needed to be done as it is with start-up ministries. It was such a blessing to serve God. My parents brought me up with the mentality to serve God and not just attend church. To this day I am uncomfortable just sitting down to hear a sermon. I'm used to being behind the microphone teaching or singing but motherhood will change all this.

Earlier that year my friend Anne headed off to the U.S. I was also heading off to the U.S. at the end of the year and I was looking forward to it. I've always been a daddy's girl. I always got so much love and understanding from him, mom was always tough with me. I envied friends like Anne that had close relationships with their mothers. Mom was just too tough and rigid for me; however she came from a tough background. People who are not shown love as a child find it hard to show love when they grow up, and I came to understand this was how mom knew how to be. The most important thing is she had a good heart and wanted the best for all her children and the best was Jesus Christ. Anything other than Jesus Christ, mom was not interested in hearing about. I could talk to my dad about anything. Even to this day he would never judge, but listen attentively and give counsel. Dad gave me several pep talks when growing up, about men. My parents had the same stance on premarital sex — it was a no-no. It wasn't endorsed by God so there was no way they were going to endorse it. Dad warned me to be careful of men. No matter how nice they seemed they were all after one thing. He told me it may not be stylish to remain chaste but it pleases God and it will please my husband. It will also please him not to have a promiscuous daughter. Being a daddy's girl, I always wanted to put a smile on my dad's face and make him proud. I knew remaining a virgin would really make him proud so I determined to stay away from anything that would lead me down that path.

I left for the U.S. and went through Virginia. I had a great reunion with my friend Anne before heading down to Atlanta, Georgia where I have been ever since. It was tough being in a new country. Yes, it was exciting but everyone spoke so fast. Eventually I got the hang of the American accent. I worked for a year before heading off to college in the fall of 2000. I joined the choir in school and also in church. Singing just fulfilled me. I dated a couple of guys but quickly discovered the only way to preserve my virtue was to stay away from dating. Dad was right after all, guys were all after the same thing. In fact, one guy I really liked told me, "You are a good girl. Your brothers are my friends. I can't date you." I was so angry at him. It was a little later that I understood what he meant. If he and I dated he would attempt to sleep with me and he wouldn't be able to face my brothers. What a gentleman he was for bowing out gracefully, but it wasn't funny at the time. I met him in church and I thought church boys would be holy and sanctified. Turns out many of them were wolves in sheep's clothing. Mom's voice always rang in my ear, "Do not be unequally yoked with an unbeliever". She knew the pain of being married to one for many years before he surrendered his life to Jesus Christ and she did not want this for any of her children. So life went on — church, work, and school. I graduated from the University of Georgia in 2004 with a degree in Speech Communication. I went on to work with Walt Disney World for a year in Florida. Living and working in Florida was really awesome. However, hurricanes were brutal in Florida that year and it was a huge reason I decided to head back to Atlanta. I returned to Atlanta in the fall of 2005 and began to work my way up in corporate America. I ended up in Clinical Research Project Management and worked in the Pharmaceutical industry for several years. Professionally and spiritually, things were going great but romantically was another matter entirely.

I am a romantic. I always have been and always will be. I love being in love, I love to love and be loved, I just love that kind of love and it was hard being around friends who dated because I wanted to be someone's love too. Also, I love hard. It's all or nothing with me. Once I open my heart to you, you are all in. This was one reason why I didn't want to date much. Giving that all consuming love to someone who wouldn't end up married to me seemed like a huge waste of time. So this was an area of my life I gave to God in total submission I was very wary of marrying the wrong person. Marrying the wrong person can destroy the plans God has for your life, and I wanted to meet my man of destiny — the man God had prepared for me. I prayed for him for many years. I specifically told God that I did not trust myself to make the right decision for a life partner. I wanted God to bring the one when it was time. I did not want to be "used goods" by the time I got to the man God had prepared for me. So I stayed away from dating. I only wanted to date the man God had prepared for me as a husband. That's what dating meant to me. I was too serious minded for casual relationships. To me dating should lead to marriage I had to do what I needed to do to keep my temple holy. I knew I was human, so why would I place myself in the path of temptation? Friends saw how I lived my life over the years and said all sorts of things like, "You are too picky!" and "How will you get married when you don't go out and you don't date?" My answer always remained the same, "I serve the Most High who created me and the universe. He knows where my husband is and at the appointed time He will introduce us." I spent time serving God and grew so much spiritually that I began to have peace about my future. Another interesting thing that happened in my walk with God, I had been in choirs all my life but I had never been a worship leader. In fact I ran away from it because shyness is something I've always surrendered to. I don't like the limelight; I prefer being behind the scenes. But my mom always told me I was born to shine and that I can't hide the light of God in me because it will always be revealed. When one of the worship leaders left the church I was attending briefly for a job outside the country, I was "discovered" and promoted instantly to lead Praise and Worship. I was so scared. My tummy was all in knots. I never did well in auditions because shyness got the best of me and my voice would get all shaky and my palms sweaty. I said, "God I love to sing but I think I'm destined to be a background vocalist because being a soloist away from the comfort of my home isn't going to happen." Well, God had other plans, I led Praise and Worship for the first time during the Sunday Worship service and the glory of God came down. I was in awe because the Holy Spirit took over. I've always loved worship. It's such an intimate experience with God where you sing a love ballad to Him. Once I was done with the praise session I closed my eyes and led the choir and congregation in worship. I wasn't aware of anyone else because I was communing with my God. Another gift was revealed that day. A worship leader was born not by my power or by my might. The pastor called for an encore right before he preached and many congregation members walked up to me after church commending me. One lady actually used the word anointed. She said it so sincerely, "You are anointed. Don't stop, please continue. You are a blessing." I deflected all the accolades to God because if it was me standing there leading worship it would have been a shaky mess but it was God who showed up through me and I gave Him all the glory.

So how did I finally meet my husband? In 2007, Thanksgiving Day was the worst holiday I'd ever had. I was alone. I had one married brother and the other two were dating and were spending Thanksgiving with their ladies. So I took myself out to a fancy Atlanta restaurant and ordered a lamb dish. I rebelled against ordering turkey. Turkey meant family, and since I was alone without family lamb it was. (Hey, I had to date myself since no one was dating me.) I came back home and sat in the dark watching *The Notebook*. If you happen to have seen this movie and you are a romantic like me, you will understand what happened to me that night. I finished the movie and was sobbing like my whole world had collapsed. I got on my knees and said "God, please hear my cry today. I have served you faithfully and separated myself for you. I will serve you all the days of my life but please take this loneliness from me. If there is anything that is in me that is preventing me from meeting my husband remove it now and if there is anything in him causing the delay please remove it now." After this prayer I was filled with so much peace and slept like a baby. When I woke up the next day, I checked my email and my friend had sent an email introducing me to her brother and she copied him on it! When I read the email, something within me said, "This is it!" but I dismissed it. I had been praying since 1999 for my husband, would God just answer me that quickly? Anyway, I replied to the email and introduced myself. I was blushing at this point because it was unexpected what my friend did. Her brother was in Nigeria so I didn't dwell too much on it. Long distance wasn't my thing. After a couple of emails back and forth. We talked for the first time a month later in December. I remember I did most of the talking. I apologized for talking too much so he could say something, all he could tell me was he was excited. That's what he kept on repeating. I was wondering what was making him so excited. He later told me he had also been praying for his wife and a prophecy had come that he shouldn't bother dating anyone in Nigeria because his wife was abroad. He was actually making plans to go to England before he got sidetracked by me. When he heard my voice he knew I was the one. The next time we talked was in January 2008 and he came after me like the fastest car in the world! I was beginning to wonder what kind of person he was. He was so determined and expressive. I told him to take it easy because I was and still am a very cautious person. I told him to go and read Proverbs 31 and that I was a serious minded woman with no time for games at all. When he read it, he saw my definition, understood my definition and loved my definition. He was now determined to marry me because he saw the value in my packaged definition. He told me, "You are a wife, not a girlfriend and whether I am ready or not, I will not let you pass me by!" I told him we really needed to pray because marriage is a destiny shaper or destiny breaker. It is very important to marry the right person. If not, fulfilling your maximum purpose on this earth will be next to impossible. We prayed and fasted and God began to speak. It was so weird and amazing. God began to synchronize us almost immediately. We began thinking the same thoughts and completing each other's sentences. A deep love and connection was established but even more special was a deeper friendship. By March, it seemed we had been together for years. This was when I knew for sure he was the one! I informed my parents immediately I came to this realization and they began to pray about it. I did not want a situation where I was blindsided by emotions. In matters of marriage I sought my parents counsel physically and spiritually, and if neither endorsed it I would respect it and abide by it.

Mom was the first one to get on board. She said it had been confirmed to her while she prayed. Did I mention mom is a firebrand prayer warrior? She takes everything to God in prayer and I mean *everything*. There was a time I was growing too tall for her liking and she asked God to put a stop to it. That's why I'm a modest 5'8 today; perhaps I would have been over 6 feet like my brothers. Her reasoning was funny. She didn't want me to have trouble meeting men. She felt if I was too tall it would prevent men from approaching me. Thank God for the foresight of mothers because I quickly grew to find out it was the petite ladies that got the way taller men. My friend Anne for instance is 5'5. Guess how tall her husband is? 6'4! Anyway, dad was understandably more cautious, but God spoke to his heart to release me. In July, my future husband came over to my parents' house and introduced himself as the man who planned to marry me. This was a man who had not met me physically yet he was so sure I was the one for him. What a brave thing to do. Sometimes I wonder how dad received him. I wish I was there to see it!

The peace of God overwhelmed us, and we knew even without having met physically that we were destined to be together as man and wife. After being away from Nigeria for nine years I had to come home to fulfill all righteousness and check out my guy. The first time I saw him it was so easy, so comfortable, so beautiful. There was no hint of shyness or awkwardness. He gave me a big hug, took a deep breath, looked deep into my eyes, and said "My crown, my wife, my all...I am holding the mother of my babies." It was surreal how God accelerated everything. I remember when my dad asked him why he wanted to marry me he didn't give a frilly love filled answer but stated quite matter of factly that he had to marry me because marrying the wrong woman would put his life off-course. I was the right one (I'm paraphrasing but that's the gist of what he said). I was very impressed with his answer because love aside, marriage is a serious matter I didn't want to be thrown off-course either.   On December 20, 2008, we celebrated our engagement with family and friends. Ten months later he joined me in the U.S. and we got married on December 12, 2009. That was the happiest day of my life. I couldn't believe it! The long-distance relationship was finally over and we now belonged to each other in the eyes of God and everyone. Another funny thing was my precious friend Anne got married on the same day so we had another thing to bond and cement our friendship. God is amazing! Those were the exciting days, reveling in the novelty of being newlyweds. Four months into our marriage we found out I was pregnant. Selfish me was appalled we got pregnant so quick. We had a two year plan — no babies until we had spent enough time with each other, but God had other plans. Our daughter was born December 29, 2010 and she was so beautiful I couldn't believe she was ours. I couldn't believe I was a mom. I wasn't quite done learning how to be a wife and now motherhood was thrown in the mix. Another part of my heart opened up to embrace this precious child we were so grateful to God for. We settled in, raising our very energetic little one. Of course by now conflicts had started to arise as it is bound to in every marriage, but I saw them as typical and did my best to live with it. I loved my husband and I was committed to making the relationship work. But I made the fatal mistake of taking God out of it. I neglected to pray for my home. I solved every problem by myself and never by the counsel of the Holy Spirit. But God was about to call me to order. And Boy! Oh Boy! Did He call me to order!

I wanted to be in love with God. I was a Christian and grew up as a Christian but I was in many ways a baby Christian. I prayed about this and it took almost a year for God to answer my prayer and He did in an explosive way. I was literally brought to my knees. I was taken to "The Wretched Place." I was broken, I was humbled, the words fail me to express how the very foundation of me was shaken. Of course when bad things happen there is always that question, Why? And God began to reveal Himself to me. He had to break me, to use me for His glory. He had to break me, so I could see how awesome He was. He had to break me, so I could stop compartmentalizing Him and instead give Him free reign in EVERY facet of my life. He had to break me, so I could begin to fulfill my God-given destiny. I wept. I wept about my brokenness and wretchedness and I wept asking Him to forgive me, for if He had not done this I wouldn't have known how lost I was. God had to break me, in order for me to see His immense love for me. God had to break me, to remove my focus from earthly things to heavenly things. I was reduced to ashes..." – Bella Alex-Nosagie, *Wisdom from God's Garden.*

Amazing Grace, How sweet the sound,
That saved a wretch like me.

I once was lost but now am found
Was blind, but now I see. – John Newton

2

The Wretched Place

What exactly is "The Wretched Place"? This is a place where God takes you out of love because you have been so blind to see how lost you are and how far away you are from His plans for you. Here, God will strip you down and break every pride in you, He will humble you and let you know you are indeed NOTHING without Him.

Wretchedness began for me in 2009 when my mom had a stroke. Mom is the strongest woman I know. She's tough love all the way, never scared to speak her mind, never scared of anything because she had Jesus Christ and knew who she was in Him. This was a big blow to the entire family. 2009 was the year I was getting married this was the time I needed my mom. I felt sad, scared, and happy at the same time. Happy because a long time dream of mine was coming true. I would be kissing goodbye to the single life that year. I also felt very guilty for being happy. She had the stroke in February 2009. Shortly before my wedding we discovered she also had stage 3 breast cancer. This was mind boggling. She lost her speech and her reflexes. The strongest person I knew was now as weak as a baby. I cried so much. I could not understand how someone who had served God so faithfully for many years could have this happen to her. This woke me up to the fact that I didn't really know God at all. I thought if you followed God trials would surely come but not like this, this was too much Lord. As I explained earlier I've always been closer to my dad because though I look like my mom there is a softness to me which I attribute to coming from a loving background. Mom is tough because she knew no other way. She was not brought up in an atmosphere of love; she was brought up in an atmosphere where she had to always prove herself and so a thick skin had developed to cover all the hurt and pain. Before I left Nigeria we had a heart-to-heart talk and she told me, "We have not always been close, I tried to do the best for you... It may not have come across well, but when you have your child you will need me and it will be a chance for us to be close." This was why my wretchedness began because who better to prepare a daughter for her marriage and motherhood than a mother? When our daughter was born I cried because I needed my mom. It was so hard. We had no help. My husband took care of everything. He cooked, cleaned, and still had to go to work. My breasts were sore from breast feeding. Recovering from a C-section was tough. I was just a mess and no mommy to help me. But God's grace saw us through. The end of 2011 I lost my job and then I knew I was really in trouble. I had worked since I set my feet on the shores of this country with only a six month break of unemployment, but now try as I must I could not find another job. We moved from a two income household to a one income household overnight, and it was very difficult.

Six months into 2012 we found out I was pregnant and this time around I really wanted a baby boy. I grew up in a household of boys. I've always been used to boys so I wanted the privilege of raising one. I asked God for this specifically and in His infinite mercy He answered. I was so very happy once I got confirmation at the ultrasound that it was a baby boy indeed and then my soul quest really began, and I knew this pregnancy was special. With this child in me I started to question my spiritual state and I did not find it satisfying. I wanted to be in love with God. I wanted to read my Bible and pray, not because I had to but because I desired to. I asked God to help me because there was an emptiness to my life. I was almost thirty years old and not close to living a purposeful life. Sure, I was a wife and a mom, but I was aching for something more. Being jobless woke me up to this fact because with all this time on my hands and no work to distract me I began to question my purpose in life. I mentioned earlier that my parents brought me up to serve in church and not sit in church. Once I became a mother I couldn't participate in the choir anymore and truth be told after a while I resented it. I resented not having help with the children while I worked for God. Serving in church always fulfilled me. I knew no other way. I had to pray to God to help me be patient in my journey into motherhood. I told God I was ready to serve Him and love Him and I needed His help. He helped me alright, but not in the way I could have ever asked for or imagined.

Woman in Crisis

After the birth of our son we both decided I should get an IUD as a contraceptive measure because even though we had decided during courtship we would have three children I needed a break. I had preeclampsia (pregnancy-induced high blood pressure) with both pregnancies and my body was not in a healthy state to have another baby anytime soon. After the IUD placement, we resumed sexual activity, but sex was very uncomfortable for me and only got progressively worse — even downright painful. I was also beginning to have weird abdominal pains I began to feel the IUD was not agreeing with me. The whole point of it was to have sex free of worry of pregnancy, but now I couldn't have or enjoy sex anymore so what was the point? Barely a month and a half after insertion I decided to take it out expecting eventually my body would return to normal. Three weeks later sex was still uncomfortable and abdominal pains were becoming more acute. So I went to my doctor and complained once more and she asked if she could run some tests, including STD tests. I gave her the go ahead, never thinking in my wildest dreams she would find anything that would prove my marriage had been breached. A week later I got the call to come into the clinic. Our family headed out to the clinic. My husband was going to drop us off and pick us later because he had an appointment in between. As he drove, I was sitting in the backseat with our two children staring at the back of his head. My heart sinking the closer we got to the clinic. What have you done to us? For the doctor to call me in, I knew it was bad news. I had birthed two babies with her and we had a rapport. If it was anything minor she would have called me and sent my prescription straight to the pharmacy. I walked in there already defeated, holding tightly onto the car seat which contained our son in one hand, and tightly holding on to our daughter with my other hand as if they could shield me from what was to come. The world stood still when the doctor informed me I had not one but two STDs! Chlamydia and Trichomoniasis. I remember gripping her hand so tight and saying over and over again "Oh, God!" When the heart breaks, it really hurts. Everywhere hurt. I was nauseous to my gut. My ears hurt. My eyes hurt. My head hurt. My womb hurt. I was hurt. I was in shock. I was stunned. The doctor kept on telling me "It's going to be okay," but life as I knew it was over. That was the end of my fairy tale, my regal Prince Charming had pushed me off the horse that was supposed to carry us into happily ever after. I was shattered. I asked her what she had not tested for. She said, "Gonorrhea, Syphilis, and HIV." I told her calmly to run those tests and that if I had any of them she should just tell me over the phone because I couldn't take the suspense of coming into her office and wondering which one I had. I was already dead inside. She wrote prescriptions for both my husband and I. Thank God both infections were curable. My husband picked us up and he asked if everything was okay I just gave him a casual answer. I had to behave normally, but my head and heart were pounding. This was not a conversation I wanted to have in the car. I wanted to look into his face when I told him the result. In that instant I hated him. I was also relieved he had not come inside the clinic with us because I was filled with shame that I was now a part of the statistic that "all men cheat" (you know there are some women who believe all men cheat, but I still choose to believe optimist that I am that there are a few good men out there). I was very much ashamed of him. How could he do this to us? In the most vulnerable time of my life after having a baby and feeling ugly when my body was so out of sorts, when I needed the security and strength of the man that put the baby in me and what had he done? With his two hands he had broken everything. The doctor told me there was no other way to get STDs. It was as if she knew he would deny it.

When we arrived home I confronted him about it my hands were shaking badly, as I basically threw the test results at him. I was so prepared for him to admit it. But he threw me for a loop when he calmly denied being unfaithful and saying there must be a mistake. Over the next few days he behaved quite normally but there was no way I could let two STDs go. I needed to find proof since I was getting no admission from him. I decided when he was at work I would go through his things and I prayed to God to expose the truth of the matter because I was not at peace. I went through his things and found out there was a side to my husband that had been well concealed. Why would the naive Christian wife have a reason to think her Christian husband was being unfaithful to her? I woke up quickly to the fact that innocence was gone and wretchedness had evolved into another painful beginning. When I brought my findings to his attention his stoic silence and few words spoken showed that the game was up. I was so angry and hurt. I remember grabbing him by the pants and saying, "Do you know what a wife is? A wife is a vessel and you have polluted this vessel!" I have never cried so much in my life. You see, when you are first made aware of infidelity, your heart wants to deny it and find any reason to say it must be a mistake because admitting the truth means you have been tragically and irrevocably deceived. I couldn't reconcile everything with the man I shared my life with but I had to because that was the truth.

I stopped cooking and cleaning, the house was a mess, and so was I. If not for our children I would have laid in bed all day or stayed away from the house, but they forced me to function, they forced me to keep on living even though I was in a cloud of depression. I took all our wedding pictures down (they had always been displayed proudly on the walls of our home). I could not relate to that happy girl who was so happy her life partner had finally come. I remember feeling so cold, empty and dead inside. I could not sleep or eat, I was a wreck. I lay my children on the bed with me gathering love and warmth from them. Their love was the only love on earth I could trust. It was the deepest betrayal; I felt used. I questioned everything, even our courtship. I questioned my beauty and I questioned my intelligence for being so fooled. I questioned my sexuality. If it was good with me, why did he step out? The very core of myself, the very foundation of me, was shaken. The ultimate betrayal that can ever happen in marriage had happened to me

- the one who did everything right. I obeyed God, stayed away from premarital sex, preserved my virginity for my husband, sought God's face before I opened my heart and agreed to be his wife. Wasn't I supposed to live happily ever after enjoying the blessings of God? **Naïve moment 1: There is no happily ever after on earth. Only by making Heaven is this possible.** My confidence in myself was gone. My security was gone. I loved this man with all of my heart, body, and soul, and this betrayal had tarnished our testimony. Sex has and always will be so sacred to me I kept my body for my husband but by doing this to me he did not appreciate the gift of me. I was broken. I can't explain in words how shattered I was. And what hurt the most was putting all my trust in him and never for an instant thinking he would do such a thing because I thought he was a Christian. **Naive moment 2: Yes, even Christians cheat on their spouses.** I thought I had prayed enough to God to bless me with a husband who would love me, respect me and honor me in all ways. I remember writing down the list of qualities I wanted in my husband and asking God especially for a man who would never, ever cheat on me. I laugh now as I recall that moment. This is what I have learned in my walk with God. You can pray for certain things, but God is the final authority. There are many who would ask how can you stay in the marriage? Are you sure God said he was your husband? All things work together for good. When you are in the storm, the pain makes no sense and you may think God has abandoned you, but that's when you need to hug God tighter and get closer to Him. *'Call to Me, and I will answer you, and show you great and mighty things, which you do not know* (Jeremiah 33:3) and that was the route I chose to take.

When infidelity happens you need a support group. You also need to know what decision you have made before you inform your support group so no one sways you. Will you stay married or not? It is preferable that God sways you if you have decided to give up. I asked my husband during the confrontation if he wanted to save the marriage and he said yes. When it happens, you want to tell the whole world he hurt me! But at the same time you don't want to because of the shame. However, you need help or you can quickly have a break down. It changes you the way you look at life. It rocks the very foundation of you. We had only been married three and a half years, it was too early in my opinion to be dealing with this mess. **Naïve moment 3: Marital infidelity can happen at any time – early on in marriage or later on in marriage.** I felt like such a failure. I reviewed all our friends that had attended our wedding and wondered who I could call to get me through this, but I couldn't tell any of them because the shame was too great. I decided to tell my pastor who had married us and a female pastor who was more than a pastor to me. These pastors genuinely loved us, and I knew this information would be safe with them. I chose to tell my parents because they would give me the sound spiritual advice I needed and also keep me strong with their love. Now, you have to be very careful who you tell initially because you are still processing the pain and some people will throw in a lot of negativity which can cause you to be very indecisive. I told my parents because I knew they could handle it as pastors, but not all parents can handle this objectively. I didn't tell my brothers because they have always been fiercely protective of me and I wasn't sure how they would react. I didn't know if they would turn against my husband and make matters worse or if they had the spiritual maturity my parents did to handle this news without condemning my husband. If you have decided to work on your marriage, I don't suggest you start a family war. Yes, they may all get to know eventually (if you choose to disclose it to them) but not initially when you are in shock and very vulnerable. You may need to generate your support group from somewhere other than your family if you want to save the marriage versus bring it to an end. Anne, my beloved friend, I had to tell. I knew she would be the right person to carry this burden with me and I was right. None of this people I told condemned my husband. Sure, they were disappointed in his behavior but they showed love, and love is needed when anybody falls. That is what Christianity is all about.

As I told each of these people, the burden was easier to bear. Carrying this alone will do you no good. Of course, I told God. I was brought to my knees and He picked me up. This was when I truly fell in love with Him for the first time. I lay down on the floor and cried out to Him in total surrender. I asked for His mercy, and told Him that I took Him for granted and placed my husband as lord over my life. I asked Him to use me for His glory. I repented for idolizing my husband and leaving God out of our marriage, always handling every obstacle by myself. I told God this was the last time I would put Him in the backseat. I asked for His help in getting through this. I asked for His strength. I asked for His will to be done through me. I prayed like I had never prayed before. I refused to get up from the floor until I felt the forgiving presence of the Lord. The scripture He dropped in my spirit was Jeremiah 17:5-10: *Thus says the Lord: "Cursed is the man who trusts in man And makes flesh his strength, Whose heart departs from the Lord. For he shall be like a shrub in the desert, And shall not see when good comes, But shall inhabit the parched places in the wilderness, In a salt land which is not inhabited. "Blessed is the man who trusts in the Lord, And whose hope is the Lord. For he shall be like a tree planted by the waters, Which spreads out its roots by the river, And will not fear when heat comes; But its leaf will be green, And will not be anxious in the year of drought, Nor will cease from yielding fruit. "The heart is deceitful above all things, And desperately wicked; Who can know it? I, the Lord, search the heart, I test the mind, Even to give every man according to his ways, According to the fruit of his doings.* It was amazing I felt for the first time a two-way communication between the Holy Spirit and me. He truly is a Comforter and He let me know almost immediately where I had gone wrong. I had put my trust in man. I had put man over God, and now I was like a shrub in the desert. I was truly wretched but there was hope. By putting my trust in God, I would flourish. I would be alright. My spiritual state was finally at peace but the physical was still a hot mess!

The next day I ran out of the house like a mad woman — no makeup on, hair barely combed. I could not stand to be in the same space as my husband. The house was like a tomb but for the sporadic laughter of our children. I drove straight to meet with the female pastor I had decided to tell. She has always been a blessing to our lives. When we had our daughter, she came over to our home and helped me bathe the baby. I was so scared to bathe a new born. She was truly a friend and a mother given to me by God, and I knew she would guide me in this. I got to her and spilled everything. I was just crying as I revealed everything to her. I told her to inform the pastor. The one thing that I heard her say that has stayed with me to this day was, "Love God." And I have found this to be true, when you are truly in love with God, He will fulfill you like no man can and that's the truth. She told me to resume cooking and cleaning because I must always play the part as a wife unto God, not to man. *And whatever you do, do it heartily, as to the Lord and not men, knowing that from the Lord you will receive the reward of the inheritance; for you serve the Lord Christ* (Colossians 3:23-24). Playing my role will please God even though my heart was in shambles. I drove back home in much better shape than before the peace of God was beginning to saturate me. He has never disappointed me or hurt me. He will never do so either. He works everything out for my good. We began counseling immediately because my husband was leaving in a month for military duties. We had to meet with the pastors to guide us through this. I found out that my husband's behavior of denial is very common with husbands who cheat on their wives. In fact, once I was educated on how this is quite a common problem in the Body of Christ I was glad my husband had decided to come to counseling. Many husbands refuse counseling out of pride and denial, and this gave me some hope that my husband was somewhat contrite. I still found this sad that infidelity is a common problem in Christianity. I was done being naïve. Infidelity had made a grown woman out of me and if this has happened to you before you understand exactly what I mean.

How You Will Feel

Infidelity makes a woman out of you. I'd always felt like my husband's baby girl but all that went out the window. Now I felt like a full grown woman with grown pains. The pain is immeasurable. Only those who have been through it can understand the pain of it. This is why I am communicating the following feelings so those who have not experienced it can get a closer look at the devastation it causes. Forgiveness is an act of will. You will need to put on your big girl panties and also your full body armor like the medieval knights of old to survive the after effects of infidelity. How do you go on? First you must decide to go on and everything else will come after.

Ashamed

You will be ashamed, no doubt about it. You will be so ashamed you will want to crawl into a hole and never see the light of day again but I had two babies to care for. I had to live for them, and I had to be strong for them. Don't be ashamed because God loves you in all seasons of your life. He will never turn away from you. For *"whoever calls on the name of the Lord shall be saved"* (Romans 10:13). Call on God when you are ashamed and He will pick you up and make you whole again. That's what God did for me. Because of Him I found my smile again.

Broken

My tears could fill buckets. I have never cried so much in my life. Crying is too small a word to express the grief that continually poured out of me. Even when my eyes were tired of weeping, my soul wept uncontrollably I could not fathom this betrayal. I could not wrap my mind around it, so I wept. Infidelity tarnishes whatever happy memories you had. You will weep because your joy in your marriage is gone. You will be broken because everything you have built together and the love you thought he felt for you has collapsed like a deck of cards. And to recover that joy only the grace of God can give it to you.

Self-Blame

It couldn't be lack of sex. This was something my dad had taught me — that when you reject your husband sexually, it's a big deal. They feel the rejection to the core of their soul. Their manhood and essence of manhood is at stake. Some have described sex as food to men and some have described sex as thirst to men. That hunger needs to be filled and that thirst needs to be quenched. As a wife you are the nurturer to your husband. Sex should never be diminished and I never diminished it. We were sexually compatible from the beginning. I wasn't the wife who would plead "I have a headache." He got it anytime he wanted it. Being a virgin all those years and over saturated with the sexual messages of the culture we live in, I had a healthy curiosity about sex and saw marriage as the ticket and freedom to satisfy that curiosity. I could not understand why he still cheated. That was an area of our life I did not drop the ball in. I was truly baffled. I blamed myself because I felt I had failed somehow with all the efforts I had made to please my husband yet it wasn't enough. We had discussed infidelity several times in our marriage. He knew my stance on it, I believed he understood and respected it yet all that was in the dust. Don't blame yourself. I read somewhere that temptation asks, "Will you?" And sin answers, "Yes I will." He made the conscious decision to cheat. He had opportunities to flee like Joseph fled from Potiphar's wife (Genesis 39:12) God always presents a way of escape when you are tempted (1 Corinthians 10:13) but you can block out the voice of God by satisfying your desires and thinking no one will ever find out. Thank God I found out. I'm so grateful God exposed it. Better to be a fool three and a half years than to be a fool for the rest of my life.

Weak

I was weak. I was listless. I'm so glad for my children they forced me to function because I wasn't inclined to do anything. But God strengthened me. *He gives power to the weak, And to those who have no might He increases strength* (Isaiah 40:29).

Numb

It will get to the point that the pain will be so much it will turn to numbness. You can't taste or feel anything. You are like a dead woman walking. You are in sleepwalking mode — alive but barely there. Your mind can't think or function, food has no taste, laughter is gone, all that resides is coldness and emptiness. But God helped me. *The Lord is my strength and my shield; My heart trusted in Him, and I am helped; Therefore my heart greatly rejoices, And with my song I will praise Him* (Psalm 28:7).

Torment

What was it about her that made you put your vows on the line? Sin is a decision. You had a choice to flee but you decided to give in. Is this how you did it with her? I mean, what on earth were you looking for, someone who can do it while standing on her head? Was it all worth it? Am I enough for you? Did you ever love me? Do you even love me right now? Do you have any respect or regard for me? These questions will torment you for a long time. Only the healing blood of Jesus Christ will save you from torment. Your identity is in God, not in your husband. God loves you. God respects you. God honors the woman that you are. God is pleased with you as you hustle keeping the home together. God finds joy in you. When the enemy comes to torment your mind, combat him with the Word of God and you will continually overcome. It was his purpose to destroy me and cripple me, but I found my strength and identity in God. My destiny was born out of the depths of my despair and I determined to lift any soul up who has been through this. You will overcome. You will survive. When you find yourself dwelling on it, cry out to God, bring out your support partner, and turn your praise on. God will step in and renew your mind. The mind of God is not filled with torment but strength and unconditional love. *And do not be conformed to this world, but be transformed by the renewing of your mind, that you may prove what is that good and acceptable and perfect will of God* (Romans 12:2).

Hatred

I am not ashamed to admit I hated him. God knows it and I know it, so why hide it? I discovered that there is truly a thin line between love and hate. In one second all the love I had felt for this man since I had known him turned to hate. Deep, sweltering hate born out of disgust for his deceptive actions. How could he go and lie in someone else's arms and come home to my arms and behave normally? How could he be so callous and selfish and careless with all we had built together as man and wife? I am attracted to people of integrity. My dad raised me to appreciate the fact there is nothing more important on this earth than your integrity and your reputation. I have always held people of integrity in high esteem. I thought I married a man of integrity but a man of integrity would not have done this. I remember a long distance dating relationship I had before I decided I was really not going to bother dating anymore. My then boyfriend had too many girls as friends on his social media page and it was a big problem for me. I was already insecure that I was not sexually active with him so he would seek relief somewhere else. Yes, naive me thought being sexually active prevents cheating. I gave him his walking papers based on just that. I told him, "You may say you are not cheating but before you make a fool out of me and cheat anyway I'm done with this relationship." God had to deal with my self-righteousness when infidelity which I have always had zero tolerance for happened in my marriage. I had to forgive even though I thought it was utterly disgusting and despicable. I had to forgive and also deal with my judgmental attitude. Christianity is love after all.

The Holy Spirit ministered to me that there is no line between hatred and the love of God. God loves His children unconditionally. Sin separates us from God but it does not ever mean God hates us. *Though I speak with the tongues of men and of angels, but have not love, I have become sounding brass or a clanging cymbal. And though I have the gift of prophecy, and understand all mysteries and all knowledge, and though I have all faith, so that I could remove mountains, but have not love, I am nothing. And though I bestow all my goods to feed the poor, and though I give my body to be burned, but have not love, it profits me nothing* (1 Corinthians 13:1-3). By hating my husband I was condemning him and I was not pleasing God by letting hate reside in me. I had to repent of this hatred and asked God to help me remove it from my heart. There was no way I would make Heaven with a heart filled with hatred. *We know that we have passed from death to life, because we love the brethren. He who does not love his brother abides in death. Whoever hates his brother is a murderer, and you know that no murderer has eternal life abiding in him* (1 John 3:14-15). I transferred all the hatred for my husband to the devil and the sin of infidelity. God was beginning to reprogram me and was teaching me to separate the sin from the sinner. Having zero tolerance for the sin of infidelity did not give me license to have zero tolerance for my husband. I had to love my husband and continually show him love. A very difficult thing to without the help of God. God helped me and that's why today I am able to still be in my marriage. Hatred is the path to divorce and separation, and God saved me from it.

Dirty

Sex has always been sacred to me. I was raised not to fear it but to appreciate it and reserve it for marriage. My romantic self believed that once I was married my husband and I would find joy in each other sexually and create our own sexual world with just the two of us. The fact that this had been breached made me feel very dirty. I felt very filthy. I felt someone else was in our bedroom mocking the way we did things. I felt violated. I felt disgusted. My husband and I obviously did not have the same view on sex and it hurt really badly. You don't mess with something that is sacred, you just don't. However, in praying about it the Holy Spirit generated compassion in my heart and educated me on something. It's the way you are introduced to sex that influences how you will treat it. Some people are introduced to sex violently through abuse so it instils fear and lack of self-worth. Some people are taught that sex is dirty or sinful and they carry this mindset into marriage. Some people are introduced to sex carelessly and casually and so they treat it carelessly and casually. This is why one night stands and other kinds of affairs exist. God did not create sex to be casual or demeaning or violent. He created it to be enjoyed in marriage and to procreate also. The only time sex is sinful is if it's done before marriage (Fornication) or during marriage with anyone other than your spouse (Adultery) and we will discuss this more in the chapter 4. This led me to pray that God would change my husband's mindset about sex and view it as a sacred act not to be shared with anyone other than me ever again.

Defeated

A woman who has been cheated on is a defeated woman because it does not matter how beautiful you are, how sexual you are, if you graduated with the highest honors, if you are the best chef on the planet. You were cheated on not for a defined reason and this in many ways will drive you crazy. Don't blame yourself. It's not your fault your husband made a selfish decision to go outside your marriage. There is nothing you could have done physically to stop him because he made the decision himself. This is why you should not walk around in defeat or as a victim. You must rise up. Find your joy in God. The only way you can prevent your husband from ever cheating on you again is to go to battle on your knees. God created him. God knows his strengths and weaknesses. Commit everything into the hands of the Lord and, my sisters, there is nothing more beautiful than when God stands for you. When you find your identity in God you will never let the evil darts of the enemy attacking areas of your life to defeat you.

Angry

I was so angry, the angriest I have ever been in my life because infidelity is so devastating and the betrayal of all I had known and loved. I was beyond angry! I really wanted to burn my wedding album. The only thing that stopped me from doing that was my daughter loves it so much. When I took all our pictures down she noticed and brought it to my attention.

That's when I knew it was important to a two- year-old to see her parents love each other. It touched me. I had to find a way to channel my anger positively. You will have a need for revenge, but the best revenge you can give is to look and carry yourself better than you ever did. My children filled my empty days. You will feel the need to reaffirm your beauty. I went wig crazy just to switch up my look. My make-up bag went through a much needed upgrade. I walked several laps on the treadmill and turned the music up to chase away negative thoughts. You will find yourself going from laughter to tears in an instant. A word, a situation, a book, a movie can remind you of the not soon to be forgotten betrayal of your marriage. It's a terrible time but the more you sink into despair, the more you are letting the devil win. Fight! Stand tall and stand up! Put on your best accessory which is a smile and know God is holding your hand through this pain. *Fear not, for I am with you; Be not dismayed, for I am your God. I will strengthen you, Yes, I will help you, I will uphold you with My righteous right hand'* (Isaiah 41:10).

Bitter

I was so bitter. One of the things I was bitter about was I felt I was made a fool of. I said, "God, what exactly did I keep my virginity for? I gifted him with it because I thought my husband would appreciate it and look what he did to me? All his dreams came true at the expense of mine. He had it made, Lord, and look what he did?" And God began to chastise me. "Your virginity is unto me not your husband. I will continually reward you for it for you separated yourself unto me. Your pride is misplaced. You should be proud that I your God kept you pure for marriage. You didn't do it all by yourself. Or have you forgotten when you handed yourself over to me asking me to keep you for your husband? I put a hedge around you so you wouldn't fall. Where you are concerned I take all the glory. Stop blaming your husband, let's work on you." Wow! That is the magnificence of The Wretched Place. God will humble you and reprogram you and rebuild you into a new creature. *That you put off, concerning your former conduct, the old man which grows corrupt according to the deceitful lusts, and be renewed in the spirit of your mind, and that you put on the new man which was created according to God, in true righteousness and holiness* (Ephesians 4:22-24). God had indeed put a hedge of protection around me because there was a period in my life men stopped approaching me for dates. When I complained to God about it, He told me why and now He had reminded me again. God removed my focus from bitterness so I could see I was also imperfect and had no right to condemn my husband but to condemn his actions instead. Ever heard of hate the sin never the sinner? That's where God took me. If not I would still be bitter right now.

Goodbye Trust, Hello Paranoia

The most valuable thing in your marriage will be gone immediately once infidelity is discovered. And rebuilding it is going to take an immense act of will and the grace of God. As a woman I already had a ton of insecurities and a very busy mind. No one can jump to conclusions faster than a woman. This act only makes matters much worse because my worst fears had come to light. There was a time months after the discovery that I had a sharp pain in my abdomen and the devil whispered, "You got an STD again. Your husband has been up to no good." You will want to check his phone. You will want to go through his stuff. You will wonder if he is where he says he is. In fact, you will want to install a GPS to track his movements. You will want to invent something that will let you know his thoughts so you can figure out if he continues to deceive you. This is where the devil takes so much joy because when you are like this, your peace is gone and you will start to hate your husband all over again. You know how I handle this? Once you have caught a cheater he or she only gets smarter about concealing their misdeeds. But you know who is smarter? God! Whenever I get paranoid I commit it into God's hands immediately. And I pray, "Father, show yourself in this matter. I nullify any ungodly relationship in my husband's life that will not please you or benefit this marriage in Jesus name. Amen." As soon as I tell God, He fills me with peace and that's why I have no need to check up on my husband. The God who loved me so much last time to expose it, will expose any evil plan of the enemy against my home because now I am not the lackluster milquetoast prayerless person I was. I am very prayerful now and I am very fierce when praying about my marriage. The devil was sitting with his legs crossed in my home without my knowledge but now he has no choice but to flee because I will never again drop the ball spiritually in my marriage. I never fail to pray for my marriage daily and I trust God answers me.

Cynical

I became very sarcastic about weddings. When I saw a happy bride and groom I would say to myself, "She's smiling right now until he breaks her heart." If you look at our wedding album you won't believe it's the same bride writing this story. If joy and happiness could leap out of the pages of a book, you would be happy just looking at us. My smile was so wide on our wedding day, the day I married the man God had created for me. I was ready to pour all the love within me on him and I loved him in such a consuming way until he betrayed me. I now believed that "in-love" feeling was just a waste of time. I saw true love as having no truth to it. When friends looked at our pictures they commented on the love they could see in our eyes. My husband and I were absolutely crazy about each other so what happened? How could someone crazy in love commit adultery? I now understood how people go from crazy in love to divorce in a second! Infidelity can make you so cynical and make you turn your back permanently on your marriage. But that is the devil's victory, God's victory is to work through it and allow Him to resurrect what you believe is dead. *Thus says the Lord God to these bones: "Surely I will cause breath to enter into you, and you shall live* (Ezekiel 37:5).

Slightly Insane

When I confronted my husband and he finally admitted it, our baby son was in my lap. I said to my husband, "I used to be happy that our son has your eyes. Eyes I love so much, but those eyes looked at me and lied over and over again and now I'm not happy anymore he has your eyes." What an insane thing to say, right? But when you are betrayed you will be hurt in places you never knew existed. At that moment I was really scared I would hate my son for looking like his father. I was scared to raise a boy that had his father's eyes. Would he deceive me like his father did? Would he do this to his wife also? The devil had his dance of victory in that moment but once God took over me all those fears became prayer points that our children would never repeat the mistakes of their parents. I broke every curse and chain of harmful repetitive behaviors in their lives. And I prayed that God would give them partners who are truly grounded in Jesus Christ so infidelity will never be an issue in their marriage.

Contemplate Divorce or Separation

I contemplated leaving our marriage. I had specifically prayed to God for a man who would not cheat on me because I knew how I felt about it. I found it despicable because sex is very sacred to me and definitely unforgivable. But God's plan was very different. Initially I was so hurt that I had the mindset of "Forget this, I'm done!" My parents are alive and well. I can go and stay with them. My brothers are alive and well, I am not alone. I don't need you either. Do you know what I did? I prayed about it. Whenever your humanity gets in the way of your spirituality, you must go to God for the answer. God did not support such a decision, He wanted me to forgive. God brought us together for a purpose. The devil wants to destroy it and he knows this is the easiest way for a wife to throw in the towel and walk away. I had to choose if I wanted to see God's power manifested and if I was patient enough to see it through or give the devil an easy victory at the detriment of my destiny. I stood up to fight and the fighting occurred on my knees in prayer. This is the way to victory. This is the way to overcome.

Stupid

Better to know now than be walking around clueless while you are continually been made a fool of. God does not think you are stupid that is why He exposed it. Men, if your wives ever confront you about infidelity and you know you are guilty, please confess immediately. Denial only makes things much worse and it adds to the feeling of disrespect, disregard and neglect because you are abusing our intelligence. Seriously, denial is no use because whatever is done in secret will eventually come to light (Mark 4:22), especially if you have a wife who fears God and seeks to please Him. Be very afraid to cheat on a Christian wife. Her Bible tells her to forgive, but the tears and pain she brings to the feet of God will make Him arise and fight for her. No man has ever won a battle against God!

Jealous

Infidelity is not something that happens overnight. It's not a situation of a woman suddenly pulling your husband's pants down and having her way with him. Both parties cultivated the attraction before the deed. Your husband knew he was attracted to this woman at any time he could have stopped the attraction by keeping away. She made him feel good. It was an escape from the responsibilities of life wife, children, bills and such. Let me tell you something — any woman will look mighty good if she does not have the responsibilities of life to cater for. You were this way before you got married, weren't you? But now you are running after children all day, running a household, and stressed out about bills and life in general. Whoever she was created a fantasy for your husband. If he gets to know the real her, he will choose his wife. Your husband chose to marry you. You have birthed children for him. You have built a home and legacy for him. You are a Queen among women. Don't let the thought of any other woman destroy your accomplishments. You have been faithful and done your part pleasing your Father in Heaven and at the end of the day that is all that matters because, dear ones, there is a life after this one. Don't let misery and pain of this world cripple you so you miss out on eternity at your Father's side. This is why you must pray for a hedge of protection over your marriage daily. Marital infidelity is a tool of the enemy to destroy the fulfillment of your marital destiny. There is a reason God brought you and your husband together, and the devil fights it very hard. Infidelity is a huge distraction of the enemy to derail you, cripple you and destroy you. This is why many divorces exist today.

Pity (Perhaps)

Infidelity is not only utterly despicable and the height of disrespect to your spouse, but it is also an immature and childish act. You may pity him because he has revealed to you that the man of the house is not quite done being a child. Marriage is for the mature the true strength in you is when you do all you can to be faithful to one for the rest of your life. Infidelity is easy and cheap, marriage is strength all the way. *When I was a child, I spoke as a child, I understood as a child, I thought as a child; but when I became a man, I put away childish things* (1 Corinthians 13:11). Pray for your husband to "put away childish things" and be the man God has ordained him to be. A man that fears God, honors his wife and loves his family.

Vengeful

I remember I wanted to slap him so hard because God knows he deserved it, but I wasn't raised that way. My husband has never put his hands on me in a violent manner so even if he had hurt me beyond words, should I now repay evil with evil? Also, once you have slapped your spouse it gets easier to do it a second time and a third time and so on because it will get to a particular point in conflict that you feel slapping or hitting justifies and reinforces your point. Some men have never been violent with their wives but all it takes is a slap from their wife and their instinct is to retaliate in kind. Domestic violence is another terrible thing many women go through but in some cases it may have started because the wife decided to start it and it only escalated from there. The most important thing to a man is respect. If you take it away from him by getting violent, violence only begets violence. Please, if you are tempted to beat on your husband and gouge his eyes out, like he has gouged your soul out, don't do it. It will make your marital problems much worse. It is so easy for the devil to creep into our marriages and this is the environment he thrives in — hurt, anger, betrayal. Some wives believe cheating on their husbands as payback will be a good thing. Don't do it. You will find yourself emptier than ever. Adultery is an illusion of the enemy as a form of escape to make you think the grass is greener on the other side but it never is. Spend time watering the grass of your marriage and build it up instead of tearing it down with deceit and betrayal. Cheating or getting violent is not the answer because neither heals. They only create more hurt. I found myself initially praying vengeful prayers. "Lord break him as he broke me. Hurt him as he hurt me. Take him to such a point of wretchedness that all he sees is you." *The wise woman builds her house, But the foolish pulls it down with her hands* (Proverbs 14:1). I had to repent from this and started to pray constructive and positive prayers to build our home. I meditated on the Lord's Prayer (Matthew 6:9-13) and two things jumped out at me "thy will be done" and "forgive us our trespasses as we forgive those who trespass against us." God's will is not for me to utter vengeful prayers. Also, I ask God for forgiveness every day how can I not extend the same courtesy to my husband? God will not hear my prayers if I remain unforgiving.

Regret

You will regret marrying him because the devil is having so much fun in your pain that he will bring the "what if" thoughts to your mind. There are husbands who will never cheat on their wives and I wished I was married to a husband like that. But every marriage has its problems. This was not the time to covet other marriages but to work on the one God had given me and get through this storm. I didn't dwell in regret too long because I consulted God before I married my husband. I remember when we sat across from our pastor before we got married and he asked us if God had confirmed to us that we belonged together as man and wife. We both said yes. He went on to tell us that this is what will save us when the storms of marriage come. If God has confirmed that we belong together then we must always rise up and fight for our marriage, despite feelings of regret or unhappiness. There is a marital destiny God wants us to fulfill and this attack of infidelity and any subsequent spiritual attack is the devil fighting it. The amazing thing is how positive this so called attack turned out to be. In the midst of brokenness, I found me. I found my identity in God. I found out why I was created. What an immense miracle that God's faithful hand remained upon me and what was meant for evil turned into something good (Genesis 50:20).

His Apology is Insincere

The words "I'm sorry" were just too simple to apologize for uprooting me. The romantic in me wanted him to get on his knees like the day he proposed to me and cling to me bawling about how sorry he was and how his actions were absolutely inexcusable and how he planned to turn things around. When he finally admitted it, I was crying and questioned why he was sitting there saying nothing when he should be on his knees begging me. He got on his knees and apologized but it wasn't enough. I felt it wasn't sincere because I asked for the apology. I wanted him to apologize profusely without me prompting him to do so. I felt he just wasn't apologizing correctly and I really thought something was wrong with me because somehow "I'm sorry" was too simple a phrase to cover all the intense pain and betrayal I was feeling. I had to give this to God. I said "Father, I don't think he's sorry. I think he's just sorry he got caught. I don't trust him. If you want us to be together, I need you to please take all these destructive feelings from me because I can't be the wife to a man I don't trust and I feel does not care for me. If he cared why did he do this to us, Lord? Why?" I wept. Oh, the devil had so much fun in that moment. Infidelity is a terrible tool of the enemy to destroy marriages because anytime your husband upsets you it will take you back to the moment you found out he cheated on you. Something as simple as him neglecting to do a household chore will make you so angry. And if you analyze it later, you find out you are actually angry about the infidelity again rather than him forgetting to do a household chore. Infidelity is an ulcer and it's also a cancer. An ulcer because it's an open wound that refuses to heal and a cancer because it spreads and destroys every joy in your life. Thank God for His grace.

When I gave this pain to God, the Holy Spirit began to minister to me and I listened. God was preparing me for my ministry. God needed to rebuild me in order to be an effective minister of His Word. All self-righteousness and pride in me was put to death. The eye for an eye Christian that I used to be was put to death (I treated people based on how they treated me). The loving of only people who loved me was put to death. Who better to empathize with other women that have been cheated on than someone who has been cheated on? Who else can know the pain and speak to the pain of infidelity than someone who has experienced it? How could I understand unconditional love and forgiveness without being dealt such a blow like this? I had to look at the bigger picture. This was more than just me and my husband. A burden was born for women who have felt this pain. Women who are in marriages and don't know how to make it. Infidelity is the death of a marriage and only the grace and power of God can resurrect it.

Grief

You will grieve for the death of the marriage you once knew, especially if you have done your part to be a faithful and loyal and ever loving wife. I suggest you do a funeral for it because the marriage you once had is over. It's time to rebuild a new one with the same man and it will take a lot of work. *I can do all things through Christ who strengthens me* (Philippians 4:13).

You see, many people don't know how devastating infidelity is. It destroys everything. Think of your best meal that you can eat on any given day and how much pleasure you derive from it. Now think again about that meal but imagine eating it with taste buds that don't work. It still looks as great as ever but it tastes like ashes in your mouth. That is what happens after the fact — everything is the same but everything has changed.

Your husband looks the same and sounds the same but somehow he is not the same because you can't reconcile the act with him, the man you thought you knew. It is a terrible, terrible thing. I am writing this book from a woman's perspective but there are also good and loyal husbands out there with wives who are being unfaithful. Infidelity is not worth it. Don't do it. Whatever is going on in your marriage, take it to God in prayer. Seek help. Get counsel. Don't cheat. That act, even if done just once, is enough to cause your spouse to have a mental break down. It's enough to send them off the deep end. It's enough to make them suicidal. The mind, body, and soul are shattered. The innocent spouse can't focus on anything. If not for God I don't know where I would be today. God picked me up from the floor. I felt the immense power of God's love for the first time in my life. He was there when I needed Him in the darkest hour of my life for this I can never turn my back on Him.

How can you minister to the broken hearted if you have never been broken? How can you understand lack if you have never lacked? How can you testify if you have never been tested? Babies have it easy but grownups certainly do not. As you grow in Christ it gets tough and it gets hard but stay focused and run the race. When you are going through tough times, keep your head up. Your story is for His glory. Encourage yourself if no one is there to encourage you and you in turn will be able to encourage others. How do you encourage yourself? Meditate on His word and turn your praise on. Weeping may endure for a night, but joy comes in the morning! Have a blessed day! – Bella Alex-Nosagie, G+ Status Update December 2013.

The Spirit of the Lord God is upon Me, Because the Lord has anointed Me To preach good tidings to the poor; He has sent Me to heal the brokenhearted, To proclaim liberty to the captives, And the opening of the prison to those who are bound; To proclaim the acceptable year of the Lord, And the day of vengeance of our God; To comfort all who mourn, To console those who mourn in Zion, To give them **beauty for ashes***, The oil of joy for mourning, The garment of praise for the spirit of heaviness; That they may be called trees of righteousness, The planting of the Lord, that He may be glorified* (Isaiah 61:1-3).

3

Chasing my Destiny

Your greatest ministry will likely come from your deepest pain.
- Rick Warren

After my husband left for military duties, I really began to
spend time with God. I needed to heal and find myself in God
because my identity as a woman, wife and mother were totally
shattered. The separation was a divine intervention for me
because I was too damaged to function properly. I needed
space, and God gave me space. I was not concerned the
infidelity had come to light a month before he left. I was not
concerned he would cheat on me while he was away. I just
wanted him gone so I could find myself. This separation was
needed to clear minds and hearts, and God did it perfectly. I
planned to find myself in God, and I prayed that while my
husband was away from his family he would truly appreciate
what he had in us and never be led to jeopardize it again. While
my husband was physically away, I had time to come to terms
with all my tumultuous emotions. I spent time with God more
than I ever did in my whole life. I hungered for His Word
seeking comfort and knowledge. I hungered for the touch of
the Holy Spirit who is truly a Comforter. I lay on the floor

several times repenting for idolizing my husband and placing him over God in my life. I asked God to activate every gift in me because I was ready to serve Him now until He called me home. I had nothing to lose, I had lost everything and the only way I knew forward was to ask God for His help. He listened and He helped me almost immediately. Suddenly words were dropped in my spirit. Memory verses I had learned as a child in Sunday school but had long since forgotten came back. Songs were given to me during my quiet time worship and, above all, writing came forth like a spring. God began to burden me to minister especially to women who had been broken. He began to speak to people to tell me what He wanted me to do. Anne was the first person to tell me about blogging. She reminded me about a gift I had never used for God. I guess she remembered from school days that I could write. She put me on my path to destiny. She said, "Bella, go and write. You are a writer. Writing is therapeutic. You will provide healing to others as you heal yourself." That same week my brother without having any knowledge of what I had been going through told me to look into blogging so I knew this was the direction God wanted me to go. I began to blog, and what an experience it turned out to be. From my little iPhone (the pen is truly mightier than the sword) I blogged about God's redeeming love and encouraged people. I got feedback from all over the world of people being encouraged by my words. I discussed The Wretched Place several times, but no one knew the details… until now. Marital infidelity brought me to my Wretched Place, but I thank God for His grace. I am alive and well and stronger than I have ever been. God will never leave you or forsake you (Deuteronomy 31:6). God is on the throne!

I quickly discovered in blogging that there were tons of women carrying this pain and shame and it only intensified my burden. The woman in me refused to be a victim and let other women feel like victims. I hurt for women, this pain I will not wish on my worst enemy if I had one. So I encouraged almost daily. The Holy Spirit would put topics in my mind, and my senses came alive. I was inspired by all kinds of things that showed God's love for mankind in our daily lives and I shared these. Within four months my blog had 3000 hits! I was amazed that people were actually reading my posts. Let me tell you this — step into your destiny today. Don't worry about if people will discover you or not. If God has placed a song in your heart, sing it. If He has placed books in your mind, write them. Whatever He has called you to do, do it. He is the one that will enlarge your coast. Don't wait for a church building before you start a church. In due time God will provide what your ministry needs. I was shocked and humbled at the testimonies coming my way from my followers all over the world about what God was using my writings to do in their lives. 3000 hits was a big number for me because I had never done this before and I had no idea that many people would be inclined to read what I wrote. With blogging God built my confidence that I truly had a gift He wanted me to use for His glory. He then took me to another level of thinking, "Why stop at blogging? Why don't you write a book and share your testimony?"

The Birth of Beauty4Ashes12:30

I had initially called my blog Beauty for Ashes but the more I got close to God He was leading me to tell His people to love Him with all their heart, soul, mind and strength according to His Word in Mark 12:30. As much as God is available to restore us and give us beauty for the ashes in life, are we ready to prioritize Him and put Him first? That's when I decided by God's leading to rebrand as Beauty4Ashes12:30. To teach people to love God and not take Him for granted. He loves all of us deeply so why don't we love Him deeply too? Healing is very important. When God heals you and rebuilds you He fills you with such love and boldness for Him. The infidelity I was so ashamed of wasn't a thing of shame anymore once God healed me. You don't share a thing of shame with the world. I am not ashamed of it and ironically I am glad for it because there is no way I would have found my ministry at this time without it happening. There is no way I would have made Heaven the kind of Christian I was. There is no way I would have walked in destiny if this pain hadn't happened. What the devil wanted to use to cripple me empowered me because I went into the embrace of my loving Jehovah Rapha, and He showed me who I was and what He created me to be. Glory Hallelujah! *You intended to harm me, but God intended it all for good. He brought me to this position so I could save the lives of many people* (Genesis 50:20, NLT). The good thing about going through this, is there is nothing I can't forgive now. I began rebuilding relationships because grudges felt trivial. If infidelity is what you think you can never forgive and God heals you, you will be able to forgive *anything*. Now things are as they should be. God is the love of my life, my counselor, my friend, my guide, and closest confidant. I tell Him everything, I prioritize Him. I made my husband my all and paid for it dearly. Never make any human being your all, not even your children because when they betray you, you will be shattered and disillusioned and possibly even suicidal if your foundation in Christ is not strong or you are not strong as a person.

Ever since he left for military duties I intensified my efforts to find a job. I truly wanted to be a helpmate in this regard and I had worked since I arrived in the U.S. so this break was not welcomed. I also missed financial independence and wanted to reestablish my self-worth. There is a need to establish self-worth and self-esteem when you have been cheated on. This is when you are on the road to recovery and finding yourself again. I applied for various jobs but I kept getting rejection letters. At a point I said, "Lord, what's the deal? I've spent so much time and energy job searching can you please open the Heavens so I can return to the workforce?" I sat down and wondered what to do next. I felt led to focus on ministry, and I was more than happy to do so. When you are passionate about something and you land it as a job, you won't feel like you are working. Since God was now my passion, ministry made more sense to me than returning to corporate America, but I still applied hoping to do both. I always thought it would be music first, but my heart was being led to write and even more so when my husband returned. Write, share your story, help the wounded hearts who are in marriages covered in shame and defeat and have no idea how to fix brokenness. I remember one time I was on the phone, disheartened and telling my dad about all the rejection letters I was getting. He counseled me to listen very seriously to him, and I usually do, being daddy's girl. He told me to stay a virgin before marriage, and I listened. He taught me about men, and I listened. He taught me about faith and God, and I listened. You think he was going to talk about my destiny and I wouldn't listen? I thank God so much for my dad. He's the best man I know. He is not perfect, but he is the best: sweet, encouraging, funny, principled and humble despite his great achievements in life and above all a man of integrity. This was a man who left the corrupt banking industry in our home country after he gave his life to Jesus Christ. As he grew in faith, he knew he could not serve two masters. Even though he refused to endorse dirty dealings as the managing director, he was working in an environment that condoned it. He had to leave in order not to compromise his faith. He resigned. That's when our family went from wealth to financial struggle overnight. I remember when the bank came and took our furniture and cars, it was a terrible day. I remember struggling to carry our second television upstairs so they wouldn't take it. The home I grew up in was unrecognizable by the time they were done. It was disgraceful and my heart broke for my dad. This was the price he had to pay for being a man of integrity. I learned integrity from my dad, and that's one of the reasons it was beyond heartbreaking when my husband did what he did. I wanted to marry a man of integrity because that's what I grew up with. I could not relate to my husband's betrayal at all. That's why God had to step in and heal me. I can talk about my dad forever. He is one of my favorite topics. The man overcame so much out of rural abject poverty to become a force in the banking world and now a fire brand preaching man of God. I am so grateful that when my life fell apart it happened in my dad's lifetime. I needed both the strength of my Heavenly Father and my earthly father to get up from the floor and be victorious.

Dad told me to sit down and write a book. This book would be the answer to my soul quest and this book would cause change in my Kingdom work. This book will cause unimaginable open doors in my life. I listened and went to work immediately. Writing and looking into setting up a publishing company. I gave myself a deadline that I would publish in 2014, come what may. Three weeks later I interviewed for a job. The interview went so well they could not hold back from telling me they liked my attitude and I had such a positive aura. I was excited and thought it was in the bag. I prayed and thanked God for it. A week later I emailed and called them for feedback, but only received silence despite being told that they were looking to fill the job before the week was over. I was disheartened once again. I called my "person" Anne. I said, "Babe, I need encouragement big time! Nothing is panning out and I need a job. I miss being financially independent. I need my self-worth back." She spoke to me and I started crying. The soul thirsts for someone who believes in them. She believes in me, always has and always will. My dad believes in me. These relationships are necessary because when you have been cheated on, you feel your husband has no regard for you as a person. It destroys whatever worth or esteem you ever had in yourself. She said, "Why are you bothering to look for a job when God has already hired you for one? All the rejection letters are God's way of telling you to go and put your story out there for the lives that will be changed by it. Sit down and write. You have the time to write after the kids are in bed. Write! Write! Write!" I just started laughing. She has the ability to make me laugh and cry because she believes in me so strongly. Thank God for Anne, and thank God for my daddy. This was confirmation. I knew what to do. First, God had dropped it in my heart and without me prompting them, my dad and Anne told me to write a book. When God wants you to do something He will send people to deliver messages to you, listen and obey. So I now knew without a doubt what I should do. I still continued to apply for jobs but I didn't stress out about getting hired anymore God had hired me, and I was ready to get to work.

Anne used the example of Tyler Perry who went from homeless to millions, starting out writing plays. I had watched his Biography back in the day, but I decided to google him and get a refreshing perspective on how he started out. The statement that changed Tyler's perspective was when watching Oprah Winfrey's talk show he was informed that writing is very therapeutic. With all the heartache from his background, including child abuse, sexual abuse, and neglect, he wrote and from obscurity we know the name Tyler Perry very well today. He releases movies every year since he exploded on the scene with *Diary of a Mad Black Woman,* one of my favorite movies to this day. From writing plays, he evolved into acting, directing, producing, movies and TV shows. All these because he put his pain to paper and wrote. I don't know what God is going to do with this book and any other book He burdens me to write. I am stepping into my destiny with faith and obedience to God. I pray this book will change the life of whoever reads it. It will lift you out of the miry depths of despair. It will make you love God fiercely and fervently because without Him you are nothing. No man should ever make you feel that without him you are nothing or dismiss you as irrelevant. God will never dismiss you. As long as you have breath in you, your life is not over. When you hit rock bottom, guess who is there to pick you up? God is. God will always be there. Even when He seems silent, He is working on your behalf.

I doubt I would have fallen in love with God if my marriage was a bed of roses. God knew how to get my attention. God knew what would break me to really see Him. What have you idolized today? What have you placed as a priority over God? Your husband? Your business? Your career? Whatever it is, God's way of showing you love and getting you to Heaven at all costs is to strip that idol from you. I idolized my husband. I loved him with every fiber of my being. He was my testimony, my answered prayer, my everything. I was so in love, in fact, I used to call him my everything. I made the mistake of putting this man over God. My spiritual life suffered. I was busy playing the submissive wife but in hindsight submitting foolishly (we'll discuss this later). When my everything betrayed my love I was broken and crumbled. Have you seen the devastation left behind after a Tsunami? That's how I felt — ripped apart and torn into shreds. I was at square zero. God was there to pick me up. God showed Himself mighty in my life. God proved He is the ultimate love of my life because when God allows hurt to happen to you, it's for your good. When man hurts you, it's never for your good it's all for his good. I thank God every day that He loved me enough to do this to me so I could establish a deeper relationship with Him and fulfill my destiny. Out of this pain Beauty4Ashes12:30 was born and God has breathed life into it by touching hearts globally with it. God be praised!

Stranger in my own Home

When chasing your destiny expect the devil to send many distractions your way. I was stronger when my husband was away because I didn't have him around as a constant reminder of how he failed me. Even though I was on the path to forgiveness, the path to forgetting was another matter. Infidelity taints everything. When trust has been broken, triggers can come about at any time to take your peace. One day we had a big argument triggered by my understandable lack of trust in him. And ugly words were said. It was the worst argument we had ever had in our marriage. Before this incident, I was very much a conflict avoider, but I determined after the fact that I would always speak my mind going forward. Keeping the peace at the expense of speaking up for what was right or what I called submitting foolishly to my husband had done nothing but defile our marital bed and break me as a person. So I decided to speak up about a matter that disturbed me and it turned into a very ugly episode. This was the day I knew my marriage was basically over. I did the only thing I could do. I handed it totally over to God. I silently stood by watching and praying. I came from love and affection, he didn't. I began to learn that this is how he has handled conflict all his life — tearing his offender apart like a wounded lion. Others may have let him get away with it but as his wife, I had enough. I was mocked and ridiculed and condemned. Everything was ripped into shreds — my skills as a wife, my skills as a mother, my skills as a homemaker, all were nothing. Previously I had always run away from conflict because what he called being blunt, I called being harsh. I grew up with a blunt mom, my goodness! Mom would say some things (and she lacked tact too!) and dad would always have to go behind her doing damage control. Whenever my mom spoke to me bluntly, I never felt like she was speaking from a place that lacked love. She was always direct but she never destroyed my self-esteem. Somehow, when my husband spoke in conflict his words were designed to cut me down and it left me battle weary. There is a way you can speak to your loved ones in conflict without tearing them into pieces. My husband had not mastered that skill set yet. That's why I was pretty much a conflict avoider in our marriage. His harsh words would reduce me to tears every time. This time however there were no tears. I was awed by the strength in me. That's when I knew, "Uh Oh! He's in trouble because his words don't have power over me anymore." I said to myself that this is what many women are going through in the world today and they are hopeless, but my hope is in God. I said, "Father, he has messed me up so much that even if this marriage ends today, I am fine without the institution of marriage. Now I don't trust any man so why make a new man pay for the mistakes of the old one? Father, you hate divorce (Malachi 2:16) so work this out for me. You specialize in resurrection, so resurrect this for me because this marriage is so dead right now. How can I love a man who I feel does not appreciate me, respect me or affirm me? I don't need this, and I didn't ask for this. He does not know how good he has it with me so Lord, thank you, for showing him. You brought us together for a purpose. Please let's not get in the way of that divine purpose. Even in this darkness I trust you, oh Lord, that you will work this out for my good (Romans 8:28)".

I now began to understand a lot of things. Every dream I had when I got married had been broken, every single one. And I needed the power of God to restore me. This was why I just gave it to God in total surrender. There was nothing more I could say or do. We had failed each other miserably and I was done. Words can hurt as much as actions, sometimes even more so because they are very difficult to forget. What I wanted from him he couldn't give me and what he wanted from me I couldn't give him. His focus and mine were totally different. We were so far away from being one, only God could step in and save us. I withdrew and retreated into the guest bedroom. I didn't care anymore. This was the first time I had ever slept in our guest room due to an argument. Other times we had conflict I didn't do this because it causes distance in marriage and opens the door for all kinds of evil to fly in, but since the evil of infidelity had already flown in, I could not care less. I needed time away to lick my wounds and empower myself in God's Word. At this point I didn't care about the marriage anymore. I was tired of always being the one seeking reconciliation. I was angry at his callousness and I had to ask God for forgiveness. Sex, really? As active as our sexual life was, it just felt empty not being emotionally and spiritually connected with my husband. The wounds of infidelity run deep and once discovered, whatever connection you had with your spouse ends. I was no longer secure in his love and I took measures to protect myself. I decided to go and take an STD test. I wanted to know the state of my body once more because all the time he had been away, despite flippant assurances that he was done being unfaithful to me, I was not going to be anyone's fool again. This action was also my determination to be done with the sexual part of our marriage because there was a huge disconnect and I was just tired of it all.

On I went to the STD clinic. They wanted me to take a pregnancy test first and scheduled the STD test for another week. But the wonderful thing is I met a counselor there. She asked me outright what was going on since I had listed on the form I was married. I told her about the initial discovery right after having our son, and I started crying. I thought I was done crying but I guess not. And she totally understood. Her husband did the same thing to her nine years and four kids into the marriage. She said to this day the man denies he was unfaithful but he brought an STD home so it was irrefutable. We encouraged each other. This woman was so damaged because like me, it came from nowhere. She stated it was the worst pain ever. She'd been divorced seven years and was trying to convince herself to go back into dating. She felt ugly and not good enough for any man because of her ex-husband's infidelity, and I cautioned her that, that's the biggest lie of the devil. Her identity is in God, not in the hands of her ex-husband. Infidelity is so devastating, especially when you give your all. May God help you stand in the storm of it. It messes so much with your mind and esteem. Can you imagine seven years later that she is still so messed up she can't move on with her life? She told me about a song that lifted her and I downloaded it on iTunes immediately — "Live Through It" by James Fortune. When I got home and listened to the song I broke down and cried because my heart hurt with so much disappointment in my marriage. The song spoke to my situation, it was as if it was written for me. A very real and uplifting song, it strengthened my resolve to write about my experience to help many women out there. Wallowing in shame and despair, you feel like you either live with it or you run away from it, but are you praying through it? I may have withdrawn physically from my husband but it was more to protect myself. I couldn't sleep with a man I didn't trust and who felt he had done enough to alleviate my insecurities. I was done with business as usual. This marriage was in a state of emergency, and I said, "Father, take over. You made this man and you gave him to me so thank you for working it out for my good." That's all I kept on thanking God for, believing according to His Word in Romans 8:28 that He will indeed work it out for my good. I realized I had not fully surrendered my husband and the marriage to God because I still worried if my husband was being true to me. Now however, I totally surrendered it to Him and refused to dwell on tormenting thoughts. Even though I had basically retreated to the guest room, I prayed and prayed for my husband. When he was at work I would go to our bedroom and speak life into our marriage, canceling every attack of the enemy. I surrounded myself with books and various versions of the Bible and encouraged myself. My life now had meaning. It had a purpose, identifying with numerous women who had been wronged like this. I decided to lay myself transparent as an imperfect woman seeking to do God's will. Out of a disappointing marriage Beauty4Ashes12:30 was born. All through this pain my joy increased in God because I felt for myself His existence. Only God could lift me out of such brokenness and despair. Only God could prevent me from repaying hurt with hurt. Only God made it possible to forgive the unforgivable. What is your unforgivable? Only God can redeem you from it and wipe your tears away.

A week later I went back for the STD test and it was embarrassing. Once again the shame was revisited on me. A nurse asked probing questions and she wanted to know why I needed tests done. As a counseling center this was normal to ask invasive questions but I just cried again and I told her, "Broken dreams. Every dream I've had is broken. I have no trust. I'm scared to have sex. I'm petrified to be sitting in front of you now wondering if you'll find anything." She went over all the STDs. My goodness! Sex is dangerous. Sex kills. Infidelity is not worth it. All the pictures and information I received made me want to keep my legs closed until my dying day. This is why cheating on your spouse is terrible. If you are considering it, don't do it. You can become a murderer just because of a selfish act. If you have any love for your spouse, when temptation comes you should flee. Better to drink from a disease-free monogamous cistern (Proverbs 5:15) than to mess with someone else's sexual history you can't vouch for. I was told that condoms provide 85% protection from contracting HIV and the percentages are much less for the other STDs. If you are thinking condoms will protect you, just put that by the wayside. Cheating is about deceit and subterfuge; therefore you cannot trust anyone's sexual health. *For the lips of an immoral woman drip honey, and her mouth is smoother than oil; But in the end she is bitter as wormwood, Sharp as a two-edged sword. Her feet go down to death, her steps lay hold of hell. Lest you ponder her path of life— Her ways are unstable; You do not know them* (Proverbs 5:3-6). Better to close the door of temptation and ask for God to deliver you.

A week later I returned to get my STD results. To the glory of God, I was STD free. I never saw that initial counselor again. I believe God led us to each other to encourage each other and for me to receive that priceless song, which was on repeat for the next four weeks of our marital standoff. I only spoke when spoken to. I cooked and cleaned like a maid, but I was done interacting. Things were very tense between us. I felt like a stranger in my own home. I kept away, and I was happy to do so. It was amazing to me how quickly my feelings died and now I understood how divorce occurs. This was the path to divorce. I asked God to intervene, but He didn't intervene the way I wanted. I wanted my husband to come up to me and apologize for talking to me the way he did and of course apologize again for cheating on me. Isn't this hilarious? God really needed to perfect His healing in me because I was still depending on my husband to heal this marriage, but it's us who break things and it's God who steps in to heal us. I spent so much time praying for my husband and my marriage. I was counseled to return to our bedroom. My vacation was at an end. Once again, I had to eat humble pie and reconcile when it was not my fault we were like this today. Christianity is so hard. It's easier to avoid people who don't love you right than to keep loving when you are not loved the way you need to be loved. I cried hot tears in the shower. I said, "Father, out of obedience to you I am going back to our bedroom. I'm not happy and I need you to give me the strength to play my part as a wife. I'm not going to apologize, but I thank you for making him apologize to me. That's my little ray of hope that he still cares as a husband." The Holy Spirit began to give me insight about my husband, "Watch him. He may not say much, but watch his actions towards you and the children. He cares for you and the children. He grew up without much love and affection. He learned to be hard. You may think he does not listen to you or have regard for you, but watch him. Take it easy with him." I obeyed and moved back into our bedroom. My husband apologized. I guess he missed me after all, even though he did a good job of not showing it. The devil is a liar! I took my home back from the hands of the devil and looked to God to see me through.

While I trusted God to keep working on my husband and the marriage as a whole, I began to focus on my ministry full force. Writing this book on the side, I would go on my social media platforms daily encouraging, sharing, and loving. New friendships were made. Lives were being restored. God was using me mightily to bring about a positive change in people's lives. Many of my followers would tell me they came to my page every day to be encouraged because life was just too hard. I would tell them I'm right there with you but loving God is the difference. I am so glad I woke up from Christian complacence and fell in love with God. I felt I had been walking around blindly all my life and suddenly I could see with so much clarity. I experienced God in a way I never had before. It was undoubtedly a life-changing experience and I am so glad to have an intimate relationship with Him now. When you are in love with God and you surrender totally every area of your life into His hands and He moves for you, it's beautiful and magnificent to behold. It makes you wonder why you didn't let go and let God, in the first place!

As long as you are alive you can always start again. It's hard but you are not dead so don't lose your will to live. God loves you never forget that and you are created for a purpose. Sometimes everything needs to be burnt so you can see exactly what your purpose is. May the flames of Heaven purify you and not petrify you. Let everything that has breath praise the LORD. Praise the LORD! (Psalm 150:6) — Bella Alex-Nosagie, G+ status update, July 2014.

And you shall love the Lord your God with all your heart, with all your soul, with all your mind, and with all your strength.'
This is the first commandment. And the second, like it, is this:
'You shall love your neighbor as yourself.' There is no other commandment greater than these" (Mark 12:30-31).

4

Overcoming the Devastation

I've learned to kiss the waves that throw me up against the Rock of Ages.
- Charles Spurgeon

How do you forgive the unforgivable?
I was the one with painful abdominal pains from chlamydia.
I was the one who experienced pain during sex.
I was the one who got a yeast infection for the first time in my life because of the harsh regimen of antibiotics to cure the STDs.
My husband had no symptoms so how do I forgive him?

And when they had come to the place called Calvary, there they crucified Him, and the criminals, one on the right hand and the other on the left. Then Jesus said, "Father, forgive them, for they do not know what they do." And they divided His garments and cast lots (Luke 23:34). If Jesus Christ could be so forgiving to those who crucified Him I needed to draw strength from Him so I could forgive also. My husband's betrayal crucified me. I felt naked, ashamed, bruised, humiliated and hung out to dry. The only person I knew who had gone through this and remained humble and loving through it was Jesus Christ. I drew strength from His

Word. Every time I fill out a medical history form I now have to disclose I've contracted STDs before. The shame and memories are revisited, but I am redeemed by the blood of the Lamb. Forgiveness is a process. It is an act of will. Choosing not to forgive may seem easier but if you plan to spend a lot of time in prayers in order to make it through you must forgive. *"And whenever you stand praying, if you have anything against anyone, forgive him, that your Father in heaven may also forgive you your trespasses* (Mark 11:25). God will not answer your prayers if you remain unforgiving. There are various tests along the way that will let you know you are still hurting or if you have forgiven completely. Let me give you an example. Sex with your husband after the discovery may be as mind blowing as ever, but there is an emptiness to it that occurs sometimes. Why? Because it has been breached by someone else. What you thought was so special between the two of you has been shared with someone else so it takes you back to the place of, "If it was so good with me, why on earth did he go with someone else?" After the betrayal the emotional high I used to receive from sex knowing that my husband loved me and I was secure in his love was utterly destroyed. It took a lot more effort to be excited about sex. What was once effortless on my part now required effort. I had to pray to God to help me desire my husband again. Sex is very physical for men, but women are made to desire sex when our emotions have been fed. What happens to your desire for your husband if he has betrayed your emotions? Women need security. Women need to be told "I love you" and feel they are genuinely loved. When we open our hearts, we open our legs. That's just the blunt truth of the matter. Marriage is that extra security that my heart and "legs" are safe with this man. I love him. He loves me. He's enough for me and I'm enough for him. When a husband makes his wife feel loved, he's got it made. Women are magnificent creatures. We have a great capacity to love, but we also have a great capacity to hate. That's why this phrase exists, "Hell hath no fury like a woman scorned". In an instant when that trust and emotional security are broken everything becomes a challenge. And sex that was freely and happily given becomes empty and would rather be avoided.

The discovery of marital infidelity is the death of the marriage. Only the grace of God can resurrect it and renew it. This is why so many people get divorced after it is discovered. Is divorce really the answer? Divorce does not take the hurt and pain away. Divorce does not prevent you from carrying emotional baggage to your new relationship. God hates divorce (Malachi 2:16) but specializes in resurrection. *Thus says the Lord God to these bones: "Surely I will cause breath to enter into you, and you shall live. I will put sinews on you, cover you with skin and put breath in you; and you shall live. Then you shall know that I am the Lord"* (Ezekiel 37:5-6). This is when your Christianity will be tested to the limit and in order to overcome and not let the devil win, you must forgive. Now is the time to practice the unconditional love of Jesus Christ. Even if you are in a situation where your husband is not repentant, you must forgive and pray for God to set his heart right. You are not the first wife to go through this and, unfortunately, you will not be the last. Yes, he made a conscious decision to cheat, but the battle is also very spiritual. You have to tackle this matter spiritually and physically. No matter how dire your situation is, God can intervene if you surrender this to Him.

Sexual Infidelity and God's view on Sexual Sin.

There are different kinds of sexual infidelity in marriage and I have put them in 3 categories:

- **Emotional Infidelity:** Sexual intercourse does not occur but there is a subtle promise it may occur in the future. This includes and is not limited to love letters/emails, "loving" or sexual texts (sexting), secretive phone calls, hanging out casually with someone other than your spouse.

- **Virtual infidelity:** Virtual infidelity can include some components of emotional infidelity. This includes and is not limited to visiting chat rooms to have "loving" or sexually explicit conversations, viewing pornography (videos and magazines), conducting emotional and sexual relationships via web cam with someone other than your spouse.

- **Physical infidelity:** Sexual intercourse occurs with someone other than your spouse.

I started with the first two because they all lead eventually to physical infidelity. Some spouses deceptively justify emotional and virtual infidelity since they are not physically sleeping around. Let me tell you how Jesus Christ defines adultery: *But I say, anyone who even looks at a woman with lust has already committed adultery with her in his heart* (Matthew 5:28 NLT). When you look at a man or woman lustfully and intentionally seek him or her out to fulfill sexual desire emotionally, virtually or physically adultery has commenced in your heart. Pornography is justified a lot, but if you look at it from Jesus Christ's perspective, it is adultery. The only one you should gratify your sexual desires with is your spouse. God honors sex within marriage, but outside of marriage He does not endorse it.

Fornication and adultery are sins God has mentioned over and over in the Bible that He does not condone. The one that should really make us stop and think is: *Flee sexual immorality.*

Every sin that a man does is outside the body, but he who commits sexual immorality sins against his own body (1 Corinthians 6:18). Sexual sin is serious. You are sinning against your own body. If we profess to be Christians and Jesus Christ resides in us why do we justify sexual sin? Fornication and adultery are rampant in the church, Christians have deceived themselves saying it's not possible to wait until marriage to have sex and God understands because He created them to have such needs. Christians committing adultery do so effectively because fornication was never a big deal so why should adultery be? Be careful! We may be in this world but we are not of this world (Romans 12:2). We are here to influence the world with the light of Jesus Christ in us and not have the world influence us. Anytime you have sex with somebody your spirit, soul and body are involved this is why God created it for marriage ALONE. You cannot trust your spirit, soul and body with anyone else but the spouse given to you by God. This is why it is even more heartbreaking when one spouse is faithful to God and another is faithless and goes into adultery. Adultery jeopardizes the spirit, soul and body of your innocent spouse. Everybody you have ever had sex with has a part of you in them and you have a part of them in you, it's called a soul tie. You have given this person or persons the keys to your destiny. You have caused unnecessary delays and malfunctions in your life by doing this. Aside from physical STDs there are also spiritual STDs. Everything available in the physical is also available in the spiritual. Every sin you commit has physical and spiritual consequences. If you struggle with sexual sin as a Christian repent and ask God to deliver you. Don't be deceived by the devil, avoiding sexual sin while single and also while married is very possible because all things are possible in Christ Jesus (Matthew 19:26).

Don't Throw me a Pity Party

When infidelity happens you wonder, "Oh no! What if our friends find out? They'll never treat us the same!" Tell them "Don't waste time throwing me a pity party I've already thrown one for myself. Use that energy to pray for your marriage instead." All marriages need prayers. No matter the state of yours today, you must pray for it so that the devil does not creep in and destroy your home. Sometimes sexual infidelity occurs even if your spouse is not seeking it so don't give the excuse of, "We are happy he will never do this to me!" Only your prayers to God can ensure your husband never cheats on you and flees from temptation when he is faced by it. There is so much power in prayer, and I came to this realization unfortunately after the damage had been done. Pray proactively for your marriage. The devil hates happy and peaceful marriages so his job is to take away your peace. I can tell you from firsthand experience infidelity takes your peace and your joy in your marriage. Don't wait until your home is on fire. Pray daily and put a hedge of protection over your marriage that nothing and no one will tear it asunder (Mark 10:9).

Based on how I have defined infidelity, all of the acts are one and the same. Don't try to justify it saying, "At least he hasn't physically stepped out on me." All of these are equally detrimental to the health of your marriage. This is not God's plan for marriage. Every vow you took on your wedding day is important to God and your spouse. Wives, I cannot emphasize this enough. You need to pray for your husbands. You may think your husband is on the up and up, but the deception is deep and well hidden. He may be living another life away from you and only showing you the side you want to see — the loving husband who tells you he loves you, who texts you messages of love, who makes love to you like you are the only woman in his world. Don't be deceived! Be watchful and prayerful. This is the biggest tool the enemy uses to destroy homes. But stand on God's promises and you will overcome. You are strong, you are the daughter of the King of Kings, and your identity is in Him. Go to battle on your knees and pray for the home the enemy wants to burn down. Pray for your husband to fear God and obey His commandments because that is the only way he will flee temptation. Pray for your husband to be more open with you this is very difficult for men to do. There should be marital accountability. You are a blessed wife if your husband can come to you and say he was approached by another woman or if he is being stalked repeatedly by another woman. If husbands can open up to their wives in such matters there won't be a lot of needless heartache. But the ego of a man loves to be stroked. How flattering it is to be approached and made to feel like the king of the world by other women. These women are destiny stealers. Sex can kill. So many women in my situation have contracted killer STDs through no fault of their own. It is so sad that husbands are afraid to be vulnerable with their wives and feel more confident being vulnerable with strange women. If only they know that this is what a God fearing wife craves to see and know not only your dreams but your fears and your weaknesses that she may stand and be the helpmate God designed her to be for you. It is in prayer that we are able to truly be helpmates for our husbands. It is in prayer we are able to shape them to be the men God ordained them to be.

Some people say men cheat because sex was inaccessible or not good at home. But cheating occurs because of emotional insecurity too. When a husband feels he doesn't have the support of his wife, he seeks this support elsewhere. Unfortunately for his wife, he gets a whole lot of support from those who prey on married men. Do you know what can fix this mess? Heart-to-heart talks. Intimate devotions with God together as man and wife. Counseling. Sometimes it's easier for both parties to express their issues if there's a neutral third party. But how many husbands are humble enough to do this? This is why God is your all in all. Another big reason that Christian men cheat which we rarely see as a reason is their foundation of faith. *If the foundations are destroyed, What can the righteous do?* (Psalms 11:3). Any Christian man that validates fornication will very easily commit adultery guiltlessly. As earth shattering as infidelity is to the innocent spouse, many times the cheating spouse sees it as a mistake similar to forgetting to take the trash out. It does not cut them as deeply because fornication has always been a part of their Christian life. I'm talking about men who speak in tongues, preach the Word, pray and fast like their lives depend on it; yet they are heavily involved in premarital sexual relationships. Sex is trivialized in many churches. In fact some don't preach about it. This is very wrong. You hear the saying "boys will be boys." It evolves into "men will be men." Where does that leave the wives? Should we live with fact that men should cheat because they can't control their urges? No way! We are created in God's image (Genesis 1:27) and if He does not endorse sex outside of marriage, He is letting us know it is very possible for men to flee sexual temptation when single and be faithful to their wives when married. There are Christian women exactly like this, that validate sexual sin. Women are also created in God's image therefore it is very possible to remain sexually pure before marriage and keep your marriage bed undefiled when married. *Marriage is honorable among all, and the bed undefiled; but fornicators and adulterers God will judge* (Hebrews 13:4). Our God is a righteous God who does not compromise His Word, His stance on fornication and adultery are the same. Avoid sexual sin, you will not make Heaven if you indulge in it. *Do you not know that the unrighteous will not inherit the kingdom of God? Do not be deceived. Neither fornicators, nor idolaters, nor adulterers, nor homosexuals, nor sodomites, nor thieves, nor covetous, nor drunkards, nor revilers, nor extortioners will inherit the kingdom of God* (1 Corinthians 6:9-10). Wives need to take a stand and pray for their husbands and homes. Stop wallowing in self-pity and misery. Instead, stand for your home before the devil burns it to the ground.

Overcoming the Devastation

When bad things happen, one of the quickest ways to overcome them and stay positive is to make notes of lessons learned.

1) **It Brings you Closer to God**

Infidelity is a crucifixion. You will need to look at the life and death of Jesus Christ to be strong and overcome. Jesus Christ was betrayed by the one who was close to Him, by the people He had come to save. He was hung on the cross for the whole world to see, the King of Kings was put to shame. The only thing that is different between you and Jesus Christ is He knew His destiny, but you didn't. Jesus Christ knew He would be betrayed, but you didn't. However, even if Jesus Christ knew He would be betrayed so terribly it was not easy to fulfill this destiny. He was in the flesh, no powers to deflect the humiliating and painful blows of humanity. This makes Him very sympathetic to your pain. This makes Him reach out to wipe your tears away and give you strength. This is why you should turn to Him. At this point there is no one else that will empathize or love you like Jesus Christ can. He was humiliated, but God honored Him and God will Honor you too. *But made Himself of no reputation, taking the form of a bondservant, and coming in the likeness of men. And being found in appearance as a man, He humbled Himself and became obedient to the point of death, even the death of the cross. Therefore God also has highly exalted Him and given Him the name which is above every name, that at the name of Jesus every knee should bow, of those in heaven, and of those on earth, and of those under the earth, and that every tongue should confess that Jesus Christ is Lord, to the glory of God the Father* (Philippians 2:7-11). This is why when those feelings of torment occur, allow yourself to grieve, but do not spend excessive time dwelling on them. You must strengthen yourself with God's Word and rise up from the ashes greater and stronger than ever before. *Fear not, for I am with you; Be not dismayed, for I am your God. I will strengthen you, Yes, I will help you, I will uphold you with My righteous right hand'* (Isaiah 41:10).

2) **It Will Make You a Prayer Warrior**

The wonderful thing about praying for someone who has caused you pain is your heart begins to soften. Prayer is a burden lifter and purges the dark parts of you as the light of God reenters. Infidelity will make a prayer warrior out of you. It is the best thing that will ever happen to you. Prayer is the key for holding your home together. Without praying for your husband and your children, you leave everything to chance. When you pray tirelessly, God hears and will stand for you. You will have uncommon favor where others are struggling. Some call it luck but this is the blessing of God. ...*The effective, fervent prayer of a righteous man avails much* (James 5:16). All I craved was a husband on fire for God, a man who would continually seek to do God's will, a man who would hold the hands of his wife and children and pray. Some things do not come ready made; some things you have to pray into being. If this husband of mine had come ready made, as I wished, I would still be a baby Christian. Now I understood why all through my life I would see women praying fervently in church like they would die if they stopped praying. I am sure dealing with marital infidelity was a large component of why they prayed like that. When I was growing up, my mom woke us up early for family devotions at 5:00 a.m. I was such a sleepy head and many times I had to stand through the devotions in order not to fall asleep. Those days are gone. All through the time my husband was away I would get up in the middle of the night praying for my marriage. Now I have discovered a love for prayer especially when I pray and I see God move. Infidelity or a disappointing marriage will definitely make a prayer warrior out of you, because there is no other way to survive it. You need the strength and power of God to overcome, and this can only be achieved through prayer.

3) You Will Learn Who the Real Enemy is

When you marry according to God's will, there is a marital destiny He wants you and your husband to fulfill. There is a reason why God created the two of you for each other. This is what the devil is fighting. When infidelity happens in your marriage, as much as you want to take it personally, it is more about your marital destiny than you as a person. The devil sets traps along the way in this world we live in that is over saturated with sexual temptation because it is the quickest way to stray and then break a marriage apart. If you are able to look at it from this perspective, half of the battle is already won! When marriages and homes are broken, imagine the devil doing a victory dance. Just as he wants to steal your joy from you, steal his glee from him! The devil is your enemy not your spouse. Your spouse was weak and fell for the traps laid down by the enemy whatever rage you feel should be directed at the devil. If you walk away from your marriage because you are taking this personally, you will miss fulfilling why God brought you together in the first place. And it is very hard not to take it personally. It is very hard to look past it, but with God's help you can. I've always loved reading, but now more than ever books became my best friend. I had to learn about forgiveness and living in the midst of pain. I learned a lot, and the books were such a comfort to me. Books will encourage you and season your life with strength and joy. Especially when the triggers happen, those wicked triggers of remembrance. You do not seek to remember the painful episode of infidelity but anything can set it off. Even though you have chosen to forgive, any little thing can take you back there. You need God's grace to dig you out because no matter how apologetic your spouse has been, it is very hard to forget the betrayal.

I am listing three of my favorite books that got me through:

- *Praying for Your Husband from Head to Toe* by Sarah Jaynes
- *The Power of a Praying Wife* by Stormie Omartian
- *Thriving Despite a Difficult Marriage* by Michael & Chuck Misja

Above all, be patient. Some prayers will be answered immediately and some will take longer. Don't lose faith, each word you pray, rebuilds the altar of your marriage and enables you fulfill your marital destiny.

4) **You Will Discover How Strong You Are**

It will enable you make a choice to be miserable or to be happy in the midst of the storm. It is difficult to be happy when your spouse is not aligned with you. It is a living hell. Don't let it cripple you. Let it empower you and use the pain of your Wretched Place to move God's Kingdom forward. Be that vessel that will turn something evil into good. Let beauty come out from your ashes. Don't dwell in the feelings I listed in chapter two. If you dwell there, you will be crippled. If you ask God to turn this test into a testimony and yield yourself to Him, great beauty will result from it. Your testimony will unlock people from bondage. I want anyone who reads this book to be empowered. This is the reason I am sharing this with you. Be encouraged, be empowered and let God rebuild you into the limitless person you never thought you were. What do I mean by limitless? Your unforgivable is your limit. What many people don't understand is not forgiving prevents you from getting to the next level of greatness. It limits you and keeps you stuck in a place of anger, bitterness, hurt, torment and pain. You are on a treadmill of negativity expending so much energy but going nowhere. But when you allow God to take over and mend your brokenness, divine beauty will result from you.

5) You Will Learn About Deliverance

Deliverance is necessary because you will feel dirty in all ways, physically and spiritually. When your husband sleeps with someone else, it's not only physically detrimental but spiritually. Even if STDs do not manifest in your body there is a soul tie. You may never meet the other woman, but spiritually she is now one with you. She has access to your home and all the blessings there in. Her problems and issues have become yours. It opens doors to various spiritual attacks in your life. You have to shut that door permanently. You can only do so in deliverance when you take authority over all spirits that have defiled the temple of God and your marriage bed. Absolute and thorough spiritual cleansing is necessary. There are churches that specialize in deliverance. Do your research and find one in case the church you attend does not offer deliverance. What if your husband does not go? That's okay. Make sure you go and stand in the gap for your marriage. God specializes in resurrection. There is nothing too hard for him. Just get out of His way and let Him have His way in your life, your home and your marriage.

Moving Forward

Infidelity is like shattering a glass. The innocent spouse is the glass, and the cheating spouse is the tool that has broken the glass. When you break a glass, sometimes you think you have picked up all the pieces but some other day you step on a shard and yell "Ouch!" That shard takes you back to the moment you broke the glass. That shard is a trigger of remembrance. The Bible says two heads are better than one (Ecclesiastes 4:9). If the glass breaks and you get another pair of eyes to help you pick up the pieces, you may not have to step on left over shards. When infidelity happens the only way the marriage can be better and stronger than before is if both the husband and wife can pick up the pieces together. When the memory is triggered for the innocent spouse, the offending spouse should step in and reassure the victim instead of discounting fears. Discounting fears is a very dangerous thing to do. In marriage, you should never discount your spouse's feelings. If your spouse says, "I'm not happy," you should care to find out why and come up with a solution or compromise so all is well in the home. In order to become "one flesh" (Genesis 2:24) you need to put the needs of your spouse above yours.

There is a part in *Diary of a Mad Black Woman* where the lead character cries out to her mother, "He was my everything!" and her mother cautions her immediately and says, "God is your everything! Don't you know He's a jealous God? He don't want no man (sic) before Him…you got the strength God gave us women to survive, you just ain't (sic) tapped into it yet!" That part gave me chills because that was me. I used to call my husband my everything, though he never did all the other things that were done to the lead actress. I felt beaten emotionally. I felt like I had been cast out, chewed up and spat out. I had to fall into the embrace of God to survive my brokenness. He is indeed a jealous God, Exodus 34:14 says, *for you shall worship no other god, for the Lord, whose name is Jealous, is a jealous God.* My husband became my priority after marriage. I put him over God. With my husband I didn't care much about anything else. I was consumed with him. He was my all. I checked with him before making a decision, I was always interested in consulting him in everything, I didn't make a move without him instead of using all that energy towards God. If you love hard like me, check yourself so you don't fall into this trap. Don't be so consumed by anything or anyone that you put God in the backseat. My husband didn't ask me to idolize him or put him on a pedestal, but my love for him did all that. That's why when he fell into sexual sin, my whole world collapsed because he was my world. But I am so grateful God set me straight. That was indeed an unhealthy way to love. The best way to love is the way God loves us. We need to seek His strength and wisdom on how to love our spouses, children, neighbors and strangers in the way that will glorify Him. I am telling you today make God your everything. This is why my ministry name has the 12:30 in it to remind me always of Mark 12:30 and to never, ever, ever, turn my face away from God again. God restored me and He can restore you also. Let the bitterness, pain and anger go and allow yourself to bask in the loving embrace and healing power of God.

The only way to truly recover from infidelity or a disappointing marriage is to fall in love with God. It may sound trite to you but it's the truth. God loves you unconditionally. He created you with so much love. And watches over you with Fatherly pride as you live your daily life. He cries when you cry and rejoices when you rejoice. When you know who you are in God, getting over marital disappointment will be much easier. Which method have you tried? Is it working? Are you in a marriage where you know your spouse constantly cheats but you've turned your face away and resigned yourself to live with it? Have you tried to forgive emotional hurts and it still takes a lot out of you? With God ALL things are possible (Matthew 19:26). You will hurt because you are human but there is a spirit part of you. When you get closer to God, you feed your spirit and the spirit becomes stronger over the flesh. Things that will ordinarily seem impossible for you to do will now become possible for you. Where you would have sorrowed previously, you find you now walk in joy.

What many people don't know is God put this yearning in us, a deep hunger to be fulfilled and He wants it to be directed towards Him. *And you shall love the Lord your God with all your heart, with all your soul, with all your mind, and with all your strength.' This is the first commandment* (Mark 12:30). God wants us to prepare for our life partners before marriage, by getting absolutely lost in Him because this is the best way we can give the best of ourselves to whoever we end up married to. God commands us to love our neighbors as ourselves (Mark 12:31) but how many of us actually love ourselves? When we look in the mirror do we love who we see or are we resigned to accepting who we see? If you love who you see in the mirror how do you treat yourself from day to day? Everybody is chasing love and wanting love and needing love but love starts with you...above all love starts with God. You cannot love your neighbor as yourself without loving God with your heart, mind, soul and strength. It is in loving God intensely that you will receive the divine power to love your neighbour as yourself. You cannot do this without the power of God. Do you love yourself? If you don't love yourself how can you love someone as you love yourself? God's love is unconditional and that's how He teaches Christians to love. I was so broken when my husband cheated on me that I was not interested in love and forgiveness. Infidelity was my unforgivable there was no way I could forgive it. When I was struggling with all the sadness and pain in my life, the Holy Spirit reminded me of a song I used to sing in Sunday school as a child, a song I had long forgotten based on 1 John 4:7-8: *Beloved, let us love one another, for love is of God; and everyone who loves is born of God and knows God. He who does not love does not know God, for God is love.* It brought me to my knees in repentance. I know God, I'm born of God, I love God, so how can I not love others? How can I not forgive even myself and love myself? Many times I believe forgiving yourself is harder than forgiving others. I was not only mad at my husband for making a fool of me, I was mad at myself for being a fool in love and trusting him totally. I hated myself for a hot minute! Forgiveness is part of love. If you don't forgive yourself, then you don't love yourself. If you don't forgive others, then you don't love others. When God became my first love after all I had been through, I began to focus on pleasing Him and making Heaven no matter the cost. Nothing in this world made sense anymore, only God and His love for me made sense. So as He rebuilt me and changed me from within, God began to reveal things I needed to do to secure my eternity with Him. I realized lack of love and being unforgiving would put my eternity with God in major jeopardy. *But if you do not forgive men their trespasses, neither will your Father forgive your trespasses* (Matthew 6:15). That set me on a determined path to please God first and make Heaven. Whatever you are clinging to that is holding you back from loving yourself and loving others, give it to God. Allow God who is love, to teach you how to truly love. To give out love even if it will not be given back to you. Your eternity with Him is not worth dwelling on who doesn't love you right or who doesn't treat you right. God is love and loves you right, let His love be enough for you. If your spouse has wronged you and you take it to God, you will see the more you pray for your marriage God will convict you of the many things that are wrong with you. The many things that are not Christ-like in you. Everything starts with you and your heart. If you have a hard time loving yourself, God will convict you that by loving Him you can love yourself. God's love gives you a new identity. This new identity is a confidence that God loves you as you are so you don't need to feel too bad if you are not loved right. Your husband is also your "neighbor" and if he has wronged you God has commanded you to love him, love him as you love yourself.

Infidelity towards God

There are too many cover ups in marriages and women are crying inside. You see the happy smiling couple out there, but when they go home they are living in separate rooms and not loving towards each other. I hope my story helps you to break down the prison you have erected for yourself in your marriage. Withholding forgiveness is a prison and you cannot progress in any aspect of your life if you remain like this. Your home is a sanctuary and should be a loving and peaceful atmosphere. Don't be a stranger in it. I am encouraging you that if someone like me can overcome, someone who always saw infidelity as unforgivable, so can you! I made a choice to make Heaven. I will not jeopardize my eternity because I can't forgive my husband. All of us have committed infidelity towards God. We do it daily in several ways. If He gracefully forgives us why can't we extend the same Christ-like behavior to our spouses, family, strangers and so forth? All have sinned and fallen short of the glory of God (Romans 3:23). Not some, but all! It is God's love that empowers you to forgive. I felt His love for me when I lay on the floor in wretchedness. When His love, and grace, and forgiveness touched me and I let Him into my life in total surrender He began to touch areas of my life I had previously not surrendered to Him. That part of my heart that held on to grudges was softened by God. His love empowered me to forgive. If you are struggling with any kind of pain in your marriage or in your life give it to God. It's only by His power you will overcome. When I told my pastor even though I had forgiven my husband, I was having a hard time forgetting. And some people say if you have not forgotten it means you have not forgiven. He told me I had forgiven but not completely so he taught me something. When you are struggling with areas of your life that do not please God, go into the Bible and search for verses that discuss it and meditate on these verses, asking the Holy Spirit for guidance to understand and receive the Word until it is a part of you. This is how you are able to begin to get past some things or what I call behaviors of the flesh. In my case it was the inability to let go of the hurt and forgive completely so I spent time studying Luke 6:27-36:

"But I say to you who hear: Love your enemies, do good to those who hate you, bless those who curse you, and pray for those who spitefully use you. To him who strikes you on the one cheek, offer the other also. And from him who takes away your cloak, do not withhold your tunic either. Give to everyone who asks of you. And from him who takes away your goods do not ask them back. And just as you want men to do to you, you also do to them likewise. "But if you love those who love you, what credit is that to you? For even sinners love those who love them. And if you do good to those who do good to you, what credit is that to you? For even sinners do the same. And if you lend to those from whom you hope to receive back, what credit is that to you? For even sinners lend to sinners to receive as much back. But love your enemies, do good, and lend, hoping for nothing in return; and your reward will be great, and you will be sons of the Most High. For He is kind to the unthankful and evil. Therefore be merciful, just as your Father also is merciful.

I realized it is the flesh, and pride in us that makes not forgiving others so comfortable. We nurse it, we hug it, and we commune with it, not seeing that it is actually destroying us.

Forgiveness sets you free and the spirit part of you that God nourishes does not dwell in hatred and being unforgiving because they are not a part of God. It is also because we are human we cannot forget. That's why the devil thrives so much in our minds rewinding the tape of pain and shame. I can tell you it does get better with time. I combat any memories by rebuking the devil and also telling God that I have forgiven and I do not want to dwell on any painful memories so He should please remove the pain of remembrance and He does. What started out as a sharp and crippling pain when memories were triggered by the devil is now a dull ache. I am trusting as I grow more in God it will eventually not ache again. I really don't dwell on it anymore, however, as I mentioned before, anything can trigger memories of your husband's infidelity. When it happens, I rebuke the devil immediately. I found my joy in God that's why I'm able to make it today. *Blessed are the pure in heart, For they shall see God. "Blessed are you when they revile and persecute you, and say all kinds of evil against you falsely for My sake. Rejoice and be exceedingly glad, for great is your reward in heaven, for so they persecuted the prophets who were before you* (Matthew 5:8; 11-12).

We cheat on God daily when we make decisions without consulting Him, when we do things that are not pleasing to Him, when we put ourselves before Him. Yet He continually forgives. That same mercy God extends to you should be extended to your husband if he has cheated on you and betrayed your love. There is a life after this one. Heaven and Hell are very real. Wallowing in keeping your heart hardened against others who have hurt you will prevent you from gaining entry into Heaven. How can you make Heaven if God will not forgive you for not forgiving others? When you look at it from this perspective, is being unforgiving worth it? It is my prayer that you decide to forgive today. Even though I am writing this book as a wife wronged by her husband, I am not assuming that there are wives out there who do not cheat on their husbands. There are good husbands who are pleasing God by honoring their wives and being faithful but the wives on the other hand are not. If you are a man and you happen to read this book, please apply the same principles to your marriage and watch God work. If you have cheated and been cheated on no matter what your gender is, give it to God today. Repent from sexual sin there is nothing you have done God will not forgive. It is only once you die it will be too late to ask for forgiveness *For the wages of sin is death, but the gift of God is eternal life in Christ Jesus our Lord* (Romans 6:23). If it is something else other than infidelity that makes you disappointed in your marriage, I encourage you to apply the principles I am discussing. The only way out of disappointment is to give it to God. Get close to God so He can empower you and restore whatever has broken the fabric of your marriage.

Love suffers long and is kind; love does not envy; love does not parade itself, is not puffed up; does not behave rudely, does not seek its own, is not provoked, thinks no evil; does not rejoice in iniquity, but rejoices in the truth; bears all things, believes all things, hopes all things, endures all things. And now abide faith, hope, love, these three; but the greatest of these is love (1 Corinthians 13:4-7; 13).

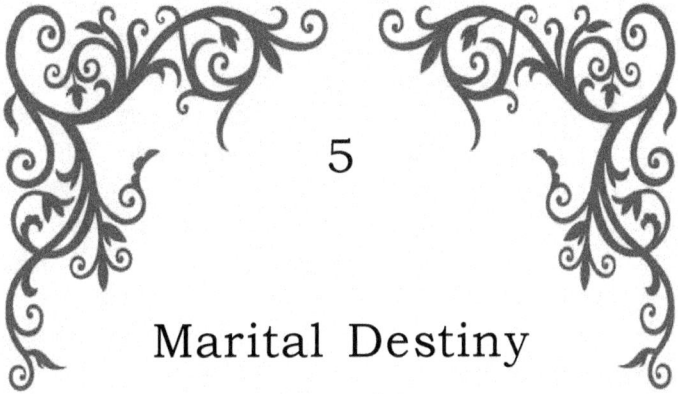

5

Marital Destiny

Forgiveness is the fragrance that the violet sheds on the heel that has crushed it. – Mark Twain

Everyone God created has a destiny to fulfill. You and I were created for God's glory and He placed talents in us to live purposeful lives and to move His Kingdom forward with those talents. There is also a destiny to be fulfilled when you get married. There is a reason why God brought the two of you together. This is why He must be consulted before you embark on marriage. God had someone in mind for you when He created you, and if you ask Him He will reveal this person to you. This is why when one of the storms of life shook my marriage I still stood in it because God clearly told me this was my husband. There is something God wants me and my husband to do for Him and I will not find this out if I walk away. *Two are better than one, Because they have a good reward for their labor. For if they fall, one will lift up his companion. But woe to him who is alone when he falls, For he has no one to help him up. Again, if two lie down together, they will keep warm; But how can one be warm alone? Though one may be overpowered by another, two can withstand him. And a threefold cord is not quickly broken* (Ecclesiastes 4:9-12). "For better or for worse, for richer, for poorer, in sickness and in health, to love and to cherish; from this day forward until death do us part..." These are the typical wedding vows taken in a Christian wedding ceremony. We say them so glibly on that day because we are full of joy and can't wait to start our lives together as husband and wife. But there will come a time you will meditate on those words and choose to honor them or discard them. I pray you honor them. Love is always much more fun in times of wealth, health and happiness. In a second, when your marriage is tested by the health of your spouse, when the finances go crazy, when your spouse cheats on you, when the worst hardships of life come upon you, what do you do? Do you stand or do you run away? Marriage is a vow between you, your spouse and God. *If a man makes a vow to the LORD, or swears an oath to bind himself by some agreement, he shall not break his word; he shall do according to all that proceeds out of his mouth* (Numbers 30:2). God honors your marriage and takes it seriously even if one or both of you don't. Christian marriages are failing all the time and it is unfortunate. 1) Do we consult God for our life partners? This is where many of us go wrong. 2) If God confirms to you this is indeed your life partner it is your responsibility to love unconditionally as Christ loves you and pray for your spouse and children continually to be filled with the love and fear of God. There is a joy in being "equally yoked" and to enjoy your marriage you have to pray for true spiritual oneness because even though you both may be Christians one can be at a much lower spiritual level and it causes conflict.

Come what may, you must be patient because not only do you have your personal destiny to fulfill, if you marry in Christ there is a marital destiny God wants you to fulfill. This is what the devil fights. God has brought you together for a purpose and if you look at your marriage with the eyes of God and not the eyes of the flesh it will cause you to endure every storm because you are focused on the end-goal. This is to encourage you no matter what your marriage is like today, no matter how your spouse views God right now there is nothing God cannot do. He specializes in the impossible. Marriage is never by your power and your might only God can carry you two. If you did not consult God before you married your spouse but you have found a relationship with God. There is nothing God cannot do. You go to battle on your knees and fight for your marriage. You pray for the heart of your spouse to be softened and receptive to God's love and commandments. You pray for the salvation of your spouse and God will do anything for your sake. In the meantime while you are trusting God to work on your spouse let God work on you so you can have the love and patience to endure. It is in marriage and family we truly learn unconditional love, this is the Heaven bound love. Conditional love and withholding forgiveness will not help us with our spiritual growth and will put our eternity with God in jeopardy. When you think of your eternity with God and your marital destiny it should enable you to stay focused and bear with each other come what may. In areas of abusive relationships please protect yourself and your children. God is not cruel for you to bear abuse while you wait for salvation to come upon your spouse. You can pray for your spouse from any location. Don't put your life at risk, instead always be wise because God is very wise. Don't give up. There is nothing God cannot do for your sake.

Becoming One

When you are married you quickly discover how the inherent differences between you and your spouse drive you both crazy. A man is a certain way and a woman is a certain way. In all the complaints of your various differences, have you ever stopped to think that you are both created in God's image? Our differences attract and repel each other but at the end of the day, we can't do without each other. If you want to know how deep and magnificent God is, how a woman looks, thinks and feels is totally different from how a man looks, thinks and feels yet we are both created in His image. *So God created man in His own image; in the image of God He created him; male and female He created them* (Genesis 1:27).

Women are driven by emotions. We fall in love with our ears. A man tells us sweet words and the job is halfway done. Men are visual, you look good as a woman and the job is halfway done. We are both sexual creatures but we approach sex differently. A woman's emotions need to be fed to enjoy and be engaged sexually. A man is visual in his approach to sex. The key for a husband to have as much sex as he wants with his wife and not have her pretend she has a headache or say, "Not tonight, Baby" is to feed her emotions. Even if you have been married for twenty years, a wife never gets tired of hearing her husband say, "I love you!" Many husbands make the mistake of assuming their wives know they are loved because they are good providers. A husband may say "Of course she knows I love her. I'm married to her aren't I? I take care of her and provide for her and the children. She knows I love her." Well, you know that saying actions speak louder than words? In marriage words are just as effective as actions. A husband should use both his words and actions to be affectionate, be compassionate and actually listen to his wife versus think she is spouting off illogically. God created women to see life from a different perspective. A husband should take time to read between the lines to decipher what his wife is saying. *And the LORD God said, "It is not good that man should be alone; I will make him a helper comparable to him"* (Genesis 2:18).

Bringing God into your Sex Life
It amazes me when married Christians don't include God in

their sex lives. They behave like God and sex don't belong in the same sentence. Excuse me, do you know that God created sex? Look at all the time He took to create our bodies and wired our bodies to find pleasure in each other. There is no sexual move you can make that God is not aware of so why not include Him when you get stumped and wonder what else you can do to make things interesting? Many Christians actively watch pornography, but as I explained in the previous chapter, it is not endorsed by God. The only sexual activity God endorses is between man and wife. Pornography arouses feelings in you created by someone other than your spouse. You may justify it by saying it's to keep things interesting in your marriage. But that is not the way. Even though you have not physically touched the person in the pornography movie your mind, heart and thoughts are polluted with him or her and that is adultery. This is why Christianity is not a religion — it is a relationship. If I am able to sit down with my parents and discuss sex, why can I not do the same with my Heavenly Father who created and invented it? The Holy Spirit is your Counselor. If things are not moving well in your marital bedroom and you are shy to discuss with your spouse, what stops you from asking God for help? He created men and women to approach sex differently. A woman's emotions need to be fed to enjoy sex. A man displays affection through sex. You find out many Christian wives are unhappy because though technically sex is good, they are emotionally starved. And the truth is no matter how good a husband's sexual skills are in marriage, if his wife is emotionally starved those good skills are like dust. Women need affection that's what keeps the fire burning for us. Couples should tune in to God and ask for His help. God wants you to enjoy your marriage and your sexual life. Don't keep Him out of it. Seek His wisdom and it shall continually be well with you.

The Waiting Room in Marriage

I have always referred to singleness as a waiting room for marriage. Truth is, when you are single you are to get busy cultivating a deep relationship with God and serving Him. You will be too busy working for God and dwelling with God to worry over your singleness. At the appointed time God will bring your life partner. This was how I spent my life when I was single. I was in the choir, I was a worship leader, and I was busy working for God. I consulted God before I married my husband and He made it clear that this was the man He created for me. Three and a half years later I am asking God how did all this happen? I married according to your will. I married a Christian too, how can this be? God's purpose for all this hurt and pain is bigger than me. A year later I can look back at this as a positive thing because it changed me to walk with God versus walking in front of Him. A year later walking in my destiny, all this hurt made sense for I cannot be a testimony without being tested. I know greater things are in store as a result of this and I look forward to how God is going to use me for His glory in the coming years.

There is also a waiting room in marriage. This is where one spouse is deeply in love with God and has fully surrendered to God and is waiting for the other spouse to get to this point so there can be spiritual oneness. With spiritual oneness, all preconceptions you both may have had about God are stripped away. Husband and wife see God for who He is and approach Him the same way. If you are in this waiting room, don't give up. Pray continually for your husband, especially when things have become so clear to you and you experience God like you never have. You have to be patient for your husband to find his way there. You yourself were lost only a minute ago. Be patient and continually pray that he is steered in the right direction where he must have an epiphany in

Christ. God can use anyone for His glory and He specializes in the impossible so don't ever lose faith. If God could change Saul of Tarsus an evil man that went around persecuting Christians into the great Apostle Paul (Acts 9), God can change your husband no matter how irredeemable you think he is. We are the ones who limit God. God has no limits. When you pray, ask and believe and it will surely come to pass. *Therefore I say to you, whatever things you ask when you pray, believe that you receive them, and you will have them* (Mark 11:24).

When God answers your prayer concerning your husband, then a new journey of marital joy starts for you where you are both spiritually one and hunger and thirst for God urgently. It is painful when you are doing it on your own, but you are only maturing and becoming the woman God intended you to be. Use this time to get close to God, pray continually for your marriage and your home, and find avenues to serve God in church and in your community. You will be too joyful in God to dwell on the lack of spiritual oneness in your marriage. God is in control and at His appointed time your husband will be touched by God.

Submitting Foolishly

Wives, submit to your own husbands, as to the Lord. For the husband is head of the wife, as also Christ is head of the church; and He is the Savior of the body. Therefore, just as the church is subject to Christ, so let the wives be to their own husbands in everything. Husbands, love your wives, just as Christ also loved the church and gave Himself for her, (Ephesians 5:22-25).

When you are submitting to a husband that largely does things his way versus God's way and you do not speak up for what is right and go along with it, this is what I refer to as submitting foolishly. If people can get in trouble for aiding and abetting a crime, how do you think God views us for not respectfully pointing out the right way to our husbands? Tell your husband respectfully that this is not right and why it is not right according to the Bible. If he refuses to see or accept it, you go to your knees and pray to God about it. Ask God to soften his heart so the right decision is made to move the family forward. And God does it. This is submitting in wisdom — taking every issue to God so He can iron it out for you. It's not for you to shout and scream and nag your husband or boss him around to see things your way. Neither is it for you to be complacent because you don't want to fight about it. It's for you to take to God so God can move him to do things right. God created your husband what seems impossible for you is very possible for God to do. Your prayer as a wife works. Don't underestimate the power of prayer. You are standing in the gap for your marriage and God respects you for it. Pray for your husband to love you as Jesus Christ loves the church. Even unbelievers are quick to quote this scripture that women should submit but what about the part that says husbands should love us? Marriage cannot be survived without God. You need the help of God and wisdom of God to submit to your husband and your husband needs the help of God to love you as Jesus Christ loves the church (Ephesians 5:25). Always keep God at the center of your marriage so you can succeed in it.

Prayer Points for your Marriage
Write down every characteristic you want to see in your husband and every positive change you want in your marriage and declare it daily.

1) Father, fill us with more of your spirit and less of our flesh in Jesus' name. Amen.

2) Father, help me and my husband (and the children you bless us with) to love you with all our heart, all our soul, all our mind and all our strength in Jesus' name. Amen.

3) Father, every relationship in our lives that does not glorify you, please remove it and cut it off permanently in Jesus' name. Amen.

4) Father, arrest any behavior in us that does not bring glory to your name in Jesus' name. Amen.

5) Father, enable us to operate with the mind of Christ at all times in Jesus' name. Amen.

6) Father, you have joined us together as man and wife let nothing and no one tear us apart in Jesus' name. Amen.

7) Father, you see all and know all. Wherever my husband is being deceitful or doing things in secret that will not please you or honor this marriage. Wash him clean, purify him and turn him away permanently from such in Jesus' name. Amen.

8) Father, please put a hedge of protection over my marriage that nothing and no one will infiltrate this marriage in Jesus' name. Amen.

9) Father, please fill my husband and I with great love for you and great love for each other. Let us stay committed to each other come what may until our dying day in Jesus' name. Amen.

10) Father, let nothing and no one remove our commitment to

you and our commitment to each other in Jesus' name. Amen.

11) Father, where there is hardness of hearts please soften and let us continually walk in love and respect with each other in Jesus' name. Amen.

12) Father, let my husband and I mutually enjoy and satisfy each other sexually. Continually keep things fresh and exciting for us and bring us closer each time we make love in Jesus' name. Amen.

13) Father, teach me to love my husband the way he needs to be loved and teach him to love me the way I need to be loved. Let the way we love each other glorify you always in Jesus' name. Amen.

14) Father, wherever there is any disconnect spiritually, emotionally, and sexually, please remove and connect us so we can indeed be one flesh in Jesus' name. Amen.

15) Father, I pray that my husband and I will fulfill our marital destiny and not deviate from it in any way in Jesus' name. Amen.

When you pray, be patient and also be expectant. God hears, and you will see Him move on your behalf. Things that were previously impossible in your marriage will now become possible. There is nothing like the prayer of a wife and a mother. As a woman you are both. Your prayer shapes your husband and your children to be who God ordained them to be. So keep at it, don't waver in your faith. See every word you speak in prayer as building a house, brick by brick. One day the house will be completed and you will move in and enjoy living in it. Prayers will make your marriage happier and more fulfilling. Stay close to God and always consult Him. He loves you and wants to help you but He is waiting for you to approach Him. Don't ever stop approaching God. He is the only one that can help you through the trials of this life, and marriage holds a good chunk of trials. The devil hates it and always attacks it. You can not fight the devil without the help of God. Love God, seek God, serve God, obey His commandments and it will continually be well with you. *If they obey and serve Him, They shall spend their days in prosperity, And their years in pleasures* (Job 36:11).

What is the future of my marriage? Only God knows. We have come a long way since this happened and I am trusting God that we will fulfill our marital destiny. Marriage is a lifetime commitment. God brought me into it and only God can release me from it. So no matter how I feel or how things are in good times or in bad times, I seek to do God's will and His will alone. God is truly amazing. Let Him into your life, all the way in so you can experience the magnificence of Him. Don't compartmentalize God and let Him into some areas and leave Him out of other areas. He is interested in every aspect of your life and seeks to help you. Don't think some things are too trivial to bring to His attention and also don't think you have a better handle on things than consulting God. Your relationship with Him will be more fulfilling if He has access to every area of your life. You can't make it without Him so surrender all, not some. God has healed me to a point that I don't regret the fact my husband was unfaithful. The irony is if he had not been unfaithful this book will not be here today helping your life. I would not have experienced God intimately. I had wasted thirty years of my life not prioritizing God, and this was a very necessary lesson for me to fulfill my destiny. This was a chance for me to see God resurrect what I previously thought was impossible — a marriage breached by infidelity. This was a chance for me to get out of the way, and watch God show me how powerful He is. Through this experience I have grown so much as a Christian, experiencing the love and power of God first hand. For the first time in my life I am absolutely sure about where I will be spending my eternity and I wouldn't trade this for the world. There is a sense of peace that I am pleasing God with my life and doing His will. Now my focus is on God and living happily ever after with Him when I die so I work hard at doing whatever it will take not to jeopardize that. I love my husband and I will love him until my dying day. It is a different kind of love now because he is no longer the love of my life. God is. I am able to love my husband now the way God intends love to be — wholesome, pure and unconditional. We have many more years ahead of us and more challenges to come. It is my prayer that we grow old and gray together and continually hold unto God's hands to see us through until He calls us home to be with Him.

~Notes~

Giving your Life to Christ

Jesus Christ died for you and me, and loves us beyond our wildest imaginations. God the Father, God the Son (Jesus Christ) and God the Holy Spirit are one in three persons. Each is a unique individual but they are all God (John 10:30, John 14:9). God the Father is the creator of the Universe. God the Son came down to earth to die for our sins. God the Holy Spirit is the Counselor and Comforter (John 14: 16-17) that dwells in us when we receive Jesus Christ as our personal Lord and Savior.

Jesus said to him, "I am the way, the truth, and the life. No one comes to the Father except through Me (John 14:6).

Let it be known to you all, and to all the people of Israel, that by the name of Jesus Christ of Nazareth, whom you crucified, whom God raised from the dead, by Him this man stands here before you whole. This is the 'stone which was rejected by you builders, which has become the chief cornerstone.' Nor is there salvation in any other, for there is no other name under heaven given among men by which we must be saved (Acts 4:10-12).

For God so loved the world that He gave His only begotten Son, that whoever believes in Him should not perish but have everlasting life (John 3:16).

If you want Jesus Christ to reside in your heart forever and always and to spend eternity with Him when you die say the following prayer:

Lord Jesus, I come to you now to present myself. Today, I have come to truly believe that you are on your throne in Heaven and that you love me. I confess to you now that I am a sinner and I am not worth being considered to be associated with you. But you are truly a merciful God, who loves all. I therefore ask you humbly to forgive me all my sins and remember them no more from today. Please have mercy on me and forgive me. Cleanse me with your precious blood and make me a new person today. Thank you for doing this for me. I desire to follow you from today, serve you and obey your commandments as written in the scriptures. So help me Lord. From today, I make you my Savior, Master, and the Lord of my life. Thank you Lord Jesus, for giving me a new life. I pray in Jesus name. Amen.

Welcome to a New Life in Christ!

Therefore, if anyone is in Christ, he is a new creation; old things have passed away; behold, all things have become new (2 Corinthians 5:17).

- Find a church to grow in and to be physically and spiritually supported.

- Read your Bible. Start from the Gospel of John to understand the ministry of Jesus Christ and His love for humanity. The Gospel of John is a more intimate and profound look at Jesus' ministry on earth compared to other Gospel accounts (Matthew, Mark, and Luke). Perhaps it is because it was written by the disciple closest to Jesus, Apostle John.

- Christianity is to be Christ-like. It's not an overnight journey as Jesus Christ begins to prune away things you have always done before that will not bring glory to His name. He is your role model. Other Christians are not because only Jesus Christ achieved perfection in the flesh. Read your Bible to understand how to be a Christian.

- Pray to Him for guidance and help, and to build a relationship. A prayer is a conversation between you and Him. He left an example for you in the Bible if you don't know how to start:

In this manner, therefore, pray: Our Father in heaven, Hallowed be Your name. Your kingdom come. Your will be done On earth as it is in heaven. Give us this day our daily bread. And forgive us our debts, As we forgive our debtors. And do not lead us into temptation, But deliver us from the evil one. For Yours is the kingdom and the power and the glory forever. Amen (Matthew 6:9-13).

Keeping your Eternity in Perspective

Christianity is about being Christ-like. The foundation of our faith is love, forgiveness and obedience to God. This is one of the reasons God sent His son to live as a human and die for our sins. An effective role model is one who identifies with you. This was the best way for God to identify with humanity. *And the Word became flesh and dwelt among us, and we beheld His glory, the glory as of the only begotten of the Father, full of grace and truth* (John 1:14).

Jesus Christ (also called the Word) left His cozy home in Heaven and came down to earth to subject Himself to mockery and brutality just for the sake of you and me. In the midst of hatred and misunderstandings, He fulfilled His ministry. Jesus Christ is our role model — not any other Christian, only Jesus Christ. I like to emphasize this because Christians can be very guilty of glorifying their pastors or any other sibling in Christ. This is very wrong to do because no human being is perfect including your pastor. The only one to achieve perfection in the flesh was Jesus Christ. Look to Him to help you in your Christian walk. There are four gospel accounts of His ministry in the Bible (Matthew, Mark, Luke and John) so you have more than enough examples of how to emulate Jesus Christ.

When you give your life to Jesus Christ you are to surrender ALL of you and lay everything at His feet. You cannot glorify God when you live in sin because sin separates you from God. When you become a Christian there is no magic wand that is waved to make you change from your old ways overnight. Yes, you are a new creation in Jesus Christ because all your sins are wiped away but it's going to be a process for you, as God prunes your sinful ways from you. Many times are you willing to let go of your past? Are you willing to let go of habits that do not glorify God?

If you are willing, ask God for help:

"Father, thank you for accepting me as your child. I am struggling with my old ways and I know they do not bring you glory. Please help me stop. Please fill me with more of your spirit and less of my flesh. Only if your spirit fills me can I overcome. I trust you Lord. I hand these over to you (list whatever you are struggling with) and I thank you for making me brand new in you in Jesus' name I pray. Amen!"

Every day I pray that God should subdue my flesh and fill me with more of His spirit. Being Christ-like is a process. Don't compare yourself to anyone because everyone's journey is different. Focus on God alone and give Him everything, including your joy and your struggles. He is very interested in you and is available to help you... but you have to seek Him out. *I love those who love me, And those who seek me diligently will find me* (Proverbs 8:17).

Being a Christian is a huge responsibility. Don't take it lightly! Salvation alone will not get you into Heaven, you must obey God also. God wants you to spend eternity with Him so you need to distance yourself from anything or anyone who will not let you be a Christian. Don't distance anyone out of hatred. It is your responsibility to pray for friends and family members who are getting in the way of your Christian walk. *Therefore whoever confesses Me before men, him I will also confess before My Father who is in heaven. But whoever denies Me before men, him I will also deny before My Father who is in heaven. "Do not think that I came to bring peace on earth. I did not come to bring peace but a sword. For I have come to 'set a man against his father, a daughter against her mother, and a daughter-in-law against her mother-in-law'; and 'a man's enemies will be those of his own household.' He who loves father or mother more than Me is not worthy of Me. And he who loves son or daughter more than Me is not worthy of Me. And he who does not take his cross and follow after Me is not worthy of Me. He who finds his life will lose it, and he who loses his life for My sake will find it* (Matthew 10:32-39). Salvation + Obedience to God = Eternity with God. Never forget this simple equation. It is only when you forsake the things of this world for God that you can make Heaven. Salvation alone will not get you into Heaven. Loving God, pleasing God and obeying His commandments; this is how to secure your eternity with Him.

God wants you to please Him and Him alone. The more you

please God, the more people will be against you because pleasing God and man at the same time is impossible. Do not put your eternity in jeopardy and compromise your faith for anything or anyone. *I know your works, that you are neither cold nor hot. So then, because you are lukewarm, and neither cold nor hot, I will vomit you out of My mouth* (Revelation 3:15-16). God is not a God of compromise but holiness and righteousness. In order to walk in holiness and please Him the price on earth will be great but your prize in Heaven will be greater. Hallelujah!

Do not lay up for yourselves treasures on earth, where moth and rust destroy and where thieves break in and steal; but lay up for yourselves treasures in heaven, where neither moth nor rust destroys and where thieves do not break in and steal. For where your treasure is, there your heart will be also. "The lamp of the body is the eye. If therefore your eye is good, your whole body will be full of light. But if your eye is bad, your whole body will be full of darkness. If therefore the light that is in you is darkness, how great is that darkness! "No one can serve two masters; for either he will hate the one and love the other, or else he will be loyal to the one and despise the other. You cannot serve God and mammon (Matthew 6:19-24).

Special Thanks

Special thanks to my G+ family. This broken bird came to you as a first time blogger writing from a place of pain to encourage and lift you up, and within four months my blog had 3000 hits! It was mind-boggling to me how quickly you embraced the entries from a very broken house wife. 3000 hits may be a small number for some but it was huge for me because when you pick up your pen and send out your words into the atmosphere and people actually read and respond, it's amazing. You never knew the details of where my writing came from but now you do. Thank you for healing me and making me believe in myself. You made me know that if I write there are people who will read and if no one else reads, you all will read because you love me. I never knew social media could be such a fulfilling outlet to find a family away from home. G+ friends, you have been good to me and this broken bird is flying high now. You played a part in helping me fulfill my destiny and I thank you from the bottom of my heart. I always say writers are nothing without readers thank you for empowering me to be an author and I hope my story empowers you to love God with all your Heart, Mind, Soul and Strength. I love you all!

About the Author

Bella Alex-Nosagie is God's Handmaiden sent to remind people in this generation whose love has "waxed cold" (Matthew 24:12) that God's love is steadfast and has the power to resurrect everything that is dead in you and around you. She is the Founder of Beauty4Ashes12:30 Publishing, LLC, a writing ministry that spreads the good news of God's unconditional love to all across the globe.

Bella received her college degree in Speech Communication from The University of Georgia in Athens, Georgia, U.S.A. before moving into corporate America and rose to the position of Global Project Manager liaising with Pharmaceutical Companies. Bella is an ordained Minister of God and is also the author of, *Wisdom from God's Garden.* Bella is married and blessed with two beautiful children and resides with her family in the United States.

Bella is always honored to hear from her readers. You can contact her directly at beauty4ashes1230@aol.com.

To learn more about Bella Alex-Nosagie and her ministry visit www.beauty4ashes1230.org.